T0016944

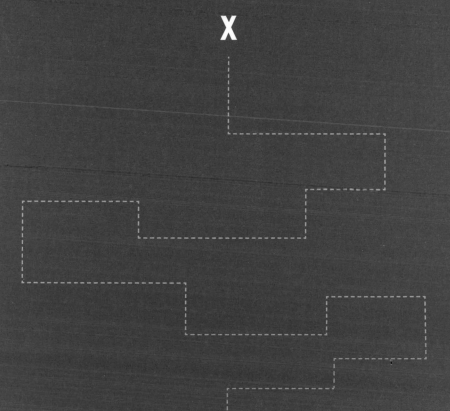

X

THE GRAND

ESCAPE

THE GREATEST PRISON BREAKOUT OF THE 20TH CENTURY

ALSO BY NEAL BASCOMB

THE NAZI HUNTERS

SABOTAGE

THE RACERS

All rights reserved. Published by Scholastic Focus, a division of Scholastic Inc., *Publishers since 1920.* SCHOLASTIC, SCHOLASTIC FOCUS, and associated logos are trademarks and/or registered trademarks of Scholastic Inc.

This book was originally published by Arthur A. Levine Books, an imprint of Scholastic Inc., in 2018.

The publisher does not have any control over and does not assume any responsibility for author or third-party websites or their content.

ISBN 978-1-338-71366-4

10 9 8 7 6 5 4 3   22 23 24 25

Printed in the U.S.A.   37
This edition first printing 2021

Book design by Maeve Norton

To Liz,
these pages would not sing without you.

LIST OF PARTICIPANTS

BREAKOUT ARTISTS:

Cecil Blain, Royal Flying Corps (RFC) pilot

David "Munshi" Gray, RFC captain

Caspar Kennard, RFC lieutenant

William "Shorty" Colquhoun, Canadian lieutenant

Charles Rathborne, senior British officer at Holzminden after
   Wyndham

Dick Cash, private in the Australian Imperial Force

William Baxter Ellis, RFC pilot

Joseph Rogers, infantry captain, member of the Pink Toes

Frank Moysey, infantry captain, member of the Pink Toes

Harold Medlicott, Royal Air Force (RAF) lieutenant

Captain Joseph Walter, 7/Royal West Surrey Regiment

Peter Lyon, Australian infantry officer

Captain William Leefe Robinson, RFC pilot

Captain Hugh Durnford, Royal Field Artillery officer

Jim Bennett, RNAS observer

Peter Campbell-Martin, RNAS pilot

Walter "Basil" Butler, infantry lieutenant

"Livewire," unnamed ringleader of the Block A escape plot

Jack Morrogh, Royal Irish Regiment major

Lieutenant Edgar Garland, pilot from New Zealand

OTHER ALLIES:

Captain Allouche, French pilot

Major John Wyndham, senior British officer at Holzminden

Lord Newton, head of the British Prisoner of War Department

GERMANS AT HOLZMINDEN:

Captain Karl Niemeyer, commandant of Holzminden after Habrecht

General von Hänisch, head of the 10th Army Corp Division, including Holzminden

Colonel Habrecht, commandant of Holzminden

Kurt Grau, camp interpreter

Mandelbrat, lieutenant to Niemeyer

OTHER GERMANS:

Kaiser Wilhelm II, German Emperor and King of Prussia

Oswald Böelcke, German ace

Baron Manfred von Richthofen, German ace, aka the "Red Baron"

Commandant Blankenstein, commandant of Osnabrück

Commandant Courth, commandant of Crefeld

Commandant Wolfe, commandant of Clausthal

Commandant Kröner, commandant of Bad Colberg

Dr. Rudolf Römer, Dutch attaché assigned to inspect German POW camps for compliance with the Hague Convention

"Stone walls do not a prison make, / nor iron bars a cage."
—"To Althea, from Prison"
Richard Lovelace, inscribed on a Holzminden cell wall

"It seems to me that we owed it to our self-respect and to our position as British officers to attempt to escape, and to go on attempting to escape, in spite of all the hardships."
—A. J. Evans

MAP OF WORLD WAR I EUROPE

ATLANTIC OCEAN

UNITED KINGDOM

ALLIED POWERS

CENTRAL POWERS

NEUTRAL

FRANCE

PORTUGAL

SPAIN

SPANISH
MOROCCO

MOROCCO

Trench warfare in World War I.

A BIT OF HISTORY

At its outset, the march into World War I looked often like a celebration. In capital cities throughout Europe, crowds poured into the streets, waving flags and singing their national anthems. Swept into this patriotic tide, soldiers mustered in their millions and prepared for war by sharpening swords, cleaning pistols, polishing boots, and readying saddlebags for their cavalry horses. Flowers garlanded their paths to trains and ships, and words such as "honor" and "glory" were spoken with reverence.

On June 28, 1914, Serbian nationalists had assassinated Austrian archduke Franz Ferdinand in Sarajevo. Although the murder lit the fuse of war, any number of acts could have stamped out the spark before the explosion, but hapless diplomats, and the leaders they served, failed to do so. Indeed, many never tried, giving in to the suggestions of battle-hungry generals. Hastening the disaster was an assembly of ossified empires, tangled alliances, inflexible war plans, massive standing armies, and the views of Germany, most prominently those of Kaiser Wilhelm II, that their country must choose "world power or downfall."

Germany intended a swift march of its armies west through Belgium, followed by a broad sweep south to envelop Paris. This decisive thrust would allow them to focus their attention on defeating Russia in the east. They made quick early progress; their huge artillery took but hours to level Belgian forts that had stood for centuries. To forestall future local resistance, they torched villages and executed their inhabitants. It was a first shiver of the horrors to follow.

The British and French slowed the German advance on Paris, then pushed it back. A series of flanking offensives and counter-offensives ensued. In the east, the Russians threw themselves against German and Austro-Hungarian troops with force. As armies of a scale never seen before engaged one another—marshaling the new technologies of rifles, machine guns, high-explosive shells, and even poison gas—deaths mounted at an alarming rate.

Many believed it would be over by Christmas. But by winter any hope of a swift victory was lost. Hundreds of thousands were already dead, on both sides, and the murder mill of the trenches had begun. Now the struggle became what some predicted it always would be—a war of attrition and annihilation that enveloped countries around the globe.

Those captured by the enemy suffered their own brand of hell.

"Those vanquished in war are held to belong to the victor," stated Aristotle, and, indeed, for most of the history of warfare, death or enslavement awaited anyone captured on the battlefield. Often their families suffered the same, their towns razed too. Brutality was strength, mercy weakness.

With the rise of professional armies in the eighteenth century, though, internment and POW (prisoner of war) exchanges became more standard. In the Seven Years' War, the French king Louis XV instructed his officers to treat the vanquished British "like your own." Nonetheless, the British and French, particularly during the Napoleonic age, ran a race to the bottom in their handling of the captured, many of whom were interned in the dark, sodden underbellies of moored ships, or "hulks." Many American soldiers in the Revolutionary War died in hulks outside New York City, "sinkholes of filth, vermin, infectious disease and despair," after being taken prisoner by the British.

Abraham Lincoln made a marked leap forward by codifying some principles of prisoner treatment in an army field manual, not the least of which stated that POWs should be given the basic needs of shelter, food, clothing, and medical attention. Then in 1899, and again in 1907, delegations from across the globe gathered in The Hague, the Netherlands, to "civilize war." Beyond stipulations on diplomacy, naval warfare, and restrictions over the use of poisonous gases and hollow-point bullets, the two international conferences set out clear rules about the treatment of prisoners.

It was forbidden to kill or wound an enemy combatant who had surrendered his arms or who could not defend himself. Prisoners must be "humanely treated" on the "same footing as the troops of the Government who captured them." Enlisted soldiers (but not officers) could be used for labor, but the tasks were not to be excessive, nor related to the war. Relief societies should be allowed to channel aid to prisoners. Germany, Britain, France, Russia, Italy, the United States, and Austria-Hungary, among many other nations, agreed to these conventions. The laundry list of dos and don'ts was so long and so comprehensive that a British international lawyer stated in 1911 that the future POW could expect "a halcyon time to be nursed fondly in memory, a kind of inexpensive rest-cure after the wearisome turmoil of fighting."

None of the diplomats gathered in The Hague in 1899 or 1907 could have anticipated the vast populations of prisoners that would come out of industrialized total war—nor the challenges this would involve. In the first six months of World War I, 1.3 million soldiers became POWs across Europe. Combatant nations struggled to confine and maintain this tide of men, and there was no sign that it would ebb any time soon. As a result, treatment of prisoners often fell short of the agreed-upon ideal. Early in the war, Britain imprisoned POWs and interned civilians in overcrowded ships, akin to conditions in the Revolutionary War almost a century and a half before. Yet despite accusations of wide-scale abuse from Germany, the majority held in Britain were maintained in decent conditions. In comparison, Russia was cruel toward POWs. Their prisoners died in vast numbers from neglect, exposure, and hard labor, many in Siberia.

Germany was also one of the worst offenders as caretakers of POWs. By mid-1916, they held 1.65 million men in a vast network of prison camps. Their treatment of the British, French, and Russians was far from the high standard of "civilized war" promised by the Hague Conventions. In the act of surrender on the Western Front, one in five British soldiers was shot or bayoneted. The moans of the wounded in no-man's-land were often silenced the same way, or men were left to die on stretchers behind the lines. Those who reached field hospitals often perished from neglect, as German doctors would frequently carry through on their Hippocratic oath only after attending to their own countrymen. Soldiers were relieved of their watches, money, cigarettes, their wedding rings, and even their boots. Individual acts of kindness occurred in these first hours of captivity, but they were far from the general rule.

Roughly 80 percent of nonofficers taken prisoner were forced to work for the Germans. Small numbers of fortunate ones, often the recovering wounded, served as orderlies in officer prison camps, cooking meals and cleaning rooms. Volunteers for these positions were easy to find. The majority suffered hard labor in *Arbeitskommandos* (working parties). They dug in the salt and coal mines, plowed fields, cut peat, split rocks in quarries, laid railroads, emptied barges, and worked in factories. They were treated little better than slaves—and flogged and abused the same. For a period, their death rates were greater than those on the front lines. According to one historian, some 50,000 Allied troops and civilians perished under such conditions.

In comparison, officers experienced better conditions. They inhabited less crowded, more solidly built prisons. They did not have to work and were even afforded orderlies to perform basic manual duties. If an officer swore not to escape, he was also allowed to take parole, or temporary leave—typically for walks outside the camp. Such was the currency of a gentleman's word being his bond and the vestiges of the old class system that once dominated all of Europe.

MAIN GERMAN PRISONER OF WAR CAMPS IN THE NARRATIVE

DENMARK

SWEDEN

BALTIC SEA

NORTH SEA

●HAMBURG

●SCHWARMSTEDT

●FORT ZORNDORF

●BERLIN

NETHERLANDS

●OSNABRÜCK

●HANOVER

●GÜTERSLOH

●HOLZMINDEN

●CLAUSTHAL

RUSSIA

●CREFELD

●COLOGNE

BELGIUM

BAD COLBERG●

●FRANKFURT

LUXEMBOURG

●MUNICH

FRANCE

AUSTRIA-HUNGARY

SWITZERLAND

ITALY

Still, imprisoned officers and rank-and-file men alike were subject to a German high command that connived against the Hague Conventions. The German army issued a handbook to its troops that called attention to the Hague pledges but included amendments about how prisoners could be put to death for insubordination, for attempting to escape, in reprisal for similar measures by the enemy, and the very broad "in case of overwhelming necessity." Their rights under the Hague Conventions ignored or abused, prisoners in Germany were abandoned to fend for themselves against commandants who had a largely free hand in how they treated prisoners, regardless of their rank.

The cruelest commandants sentenced prisoners to months of solitary confinement in small, vermin-infested cells. They inflicted beatings and innumerable petty humiliations. They allowed men to starve and their wounds to fester. They dispersed prisoners with bayonet charges. They shot at the defenseless, at times in cold-blooded murder.

Most prisoners endured these abuses—and their despair at being unable to rejoin the fight against the enemy—without ambitions to escape. Some, a small minority, decided that breaking out of these terrible prisons was a necessity worth any risk. A rare few succeeded.

PROLOGUE

HOLZMINDEN, 1918.

Twenty-seven-year-old Lieutenant Caspar Kennard was the number-one man, the digger, this afternoon. He wriggled through the eighteen-inch-diameter tunnel, a hundred feet from its entrance. In one hand he held a flickering candle, its light casting a devilish dance of shadows about him. With the other hand, he clawed at the dirt to drag himself forward. Roped to his leg was a shallow bin to bring out the excavated earth. Finally, after almost thirty minutes of crawling, he reached the end of the burrow. He scooped out a shelf in the mud wall, set down the candle, and briefly watched the flame struggle to survive in the oxygen-starved air. He took a breath, calmed himself best as he could, then started digging into the firm mix of stone and yellow clay.

Far behind him, at the mouth of the tunnel underneath a narrow paneled staircase, David Gray, the number-two man, muscled the bellows and pumped air down to Kennard. Behind Gray, the number-three man, Cecil Blain, waited to haul out the bin and pack the earth into the steadily shrinking space under the stairs. Each shift they rotated the jobs. Nobody liked to be the digger.

Tunneling was a nasty business. Kennard barely had space to shift his body. The burrow reeked of stale air, mildew, sweat, and rot. There were rats, worms, and other creepy-crawlies, and never enough air to breathe. He was always banging his head against stones, and earth pressed on him in every direction, threatening to collapse and snuff out his life. Given his lifelong fear of confined spaces, Kennard had to force himself not to panic.

Inch by inch, he carved out a small stretch of tunnel, then he contorted his body to fill the bin with dirt and rocks. There was months more of this mole work ahead, months more of digging what was either a very long tomb or a path to freedom from Holzminden, the notorious German prison camp in which they were all incarcerated. Once beyond the walls of this land-locked Alcatraz—if they made it that far—he and his fellow prisoners would have to make a 150-mile journey by foot through enemy territory to the border. The Germans would assuredly launch a manhunt, and they could face recapture—or a bullet—at any turn.

When not risking their own death tunneling underground, the men forged documents, smuggled in supplies, bribed guards for intelligence, and developed their cover stories for their flight to free Holland. To succeed would defy every odd against them.

CHAPTER 1

The sky lightened from gray to pink as the 70th Squadron of the Royal Flying Corps (RFC) prepared to take off from their base. Already the din of shelling sounded in the distance. It was August 7, 1916, at Fienvillers, France, 20 miles from the Somme battlefront. "Contact, sir!" called the mechanic, his hand on the black walnut propeller of a Sopwith 1½ Strutter biplane. "Contact!" answered its pilot, Cecil Blain, from the open fore cockpit.

Blain pushed the throttle halfway, allowing fuel to rush into the nine-cylinder rotary engine. The mechanic jerked the propeller downward, counterclockwise. With a belch of blue smoke, the Sopwith sputtered to life. The rush of air from the spinning propeller flattened the airfield's grass behind the tailplane. Seated in the aft cockpit behind Blain was Charles Griffiths, the observer, whose various tasks included radio communication, aerial reconnaissance, and manning the guns. Once they finished their flight checks, Blain waved his arm fore and aft, and the mechanic yanked out the wooden chocks securing the biplane's wheels in place.

All of nineteen years of age, the youngest pilot in his squadron, Blain might well have stepped straight off a Hollywood silent movie screen—with his square shoulders, handsome boyish face, and sweep of blond hair. He sported a thick leather jacket with fur-lined collar over a woolen pullover and two layers of underclothes. These were worn with heavy boots, gloves, and a white silk scarf. His face was slathered with whale oil and covered by a balaclava and goggles. He would need all that protection to withstand the cold at 10,000 feet.

After his squadron commander took off, Blain moved his Sopwith onto the runway. Following a quick look over his shoulder to check Griffiths was ready, Blain directed the Sopwith forward. Its red, white, and blue roundels struck in sharp relief against the mud-green fuselage. Throttle full open now, engine buzzing, the biplane picked up momentum. Blain fought against the crosswinds buffeting the wings and the inclination of the plane's nose to lift up too early. When they reached flying speed, he pulled back the stick, and the Sopwith's wheels lifted free from the ground.

Banking eastward, they soon left behind the bundle of ramshackle cottages and simple church that made up the village of Fienvillers. Once assembled in a V-shaped formation, the five Sopwiths set off eastward, the sky emblazoned bright orange ahead. Their mission was reconnaissance of Maubeuge, deep behind German enemy lines, to locate some munitions factories and investigate whether an airship base was housing Zeppelins.

For a moment, Blain and Griffiths enjoyed the thrill of soaring through the open air. The horizons stretched out in every direction. Mists clung to the low hollows of the hills, and chimney smoke rose from the surrounding villages. Compared to their maps—main roads clearly delineated in red, railways in black,

The young Cecil Blain's first RFC photo.

forests in green—the French countryside was an endless patchwork of colored fields threaded with gray lines and shadowed by clouds.

They approached the trenches of the Western Front, no mistaking their position. One airman described the sight: "Open for us to inspect were all the secrets of this waste of tortured soil, a barrier along which millions of armed men crouched in foul trenches . . . Below us lay displayed the zigzagging entrenchments, the wriggling communications to the rear, the untidy belts of rusty wire." Few accounts told of the innumerable dead rotting in no-man's-land, but they would have been visible to the pilots who passed overhead.

On July 1, 1916, shortly after Blain arrived in France, seventeen Allied divisions had begun a massive offensive to break through German lines on the upper reaches of the river Somme. At "Zero Hour," 7:30 a.m., to the sound of whistles blowing, lines of khaki-clad British soldiers and their blue-gray uniformed French counterparts rose from their trenches and attacked the Germans through no-man's-land, under the withering chatter of machine-gun fire. On the offensive's first day the Allies took but a "bite" out of the enemy's ruined line—at the cost of almost 20,000 British dead and double this figure in wounded: the greatest loss of life in a single day in the country's military history. In the weeks that followed, wave after wave of attack and counterattack resettled the lines, largely to where they had started.

As the five Sopwiths traveled across no-man's-land, suddenly the sky went thick with coughs of black smoke. *Archie!*

Nicknamed by pilots after a popular London music-hall song—whose refrain went, *"Archibald! Certainly not!"*—these shells delivered death in many ways. A direct hit would crumple a plane in an instant, sending it in a precipitous drop from the sky, like a bird downed by a shotgun. Simply being near the explosion could hurl a plane into an irrecoverable spiral. And Archie shells could kill entire aircrews with a 360-degree spray of shrapnel that tore through flesh and the fragile structures that kept the planes aloft.

A British and German dogfight. The British plane is in the foreground, with a German plane on its tail and three other planes visible in the distance.

A shell rocked one plane on the port side of their formation, but its pilot recovered. Another cut confetti-sized slits into the wings of Blain's plane, and shrapnel pinged against his engine cowling. The *wouft-wouft-wouft* of Archies pounding in his ears, Blain inspected his controls. Everything looked okay. He glanced back at Griffiths, and they shared a thumbs-up. As quickly as the barrage began, it ended. They flew on toward Maubeuge to continue their reconnaissance. Now that they were beyond enemy lines, Blain knew that fighter planes were likely to attack, and there was little cloud cover in which to hide. Griffiths readied at his mounted Lewis machine gun, and they both searched the sky.

Sixty miles behind enemy lines, they sighted the glint of sun off the river Sambre and reached Maubeuge. The ancient city had been besieged and sacked many times over the centuries, handed between French, Spanish, and Austrian dukes and counts almost too many times to count. But it had never suffered the kind of heavy artillery bombardment unleashed by the Germans. Its fortress walls were spilled piles of rubble. The planes broke away from the formation to begin their reconnaissance. Cutting across the city, Blain and Griffiths looked for the airship base marked on their maps. They passed the train station, puffs of steam from a departing locomotive rising into the air.

The mammoth gray sheds were easy to spot. On his first pass, Blain didn't see anything, but the Zeppelins could well be inside. He banked around and descended low for a second look, easing back on the throttle. In that moment, a spout of blue flame burst from the engine. One of the intake valves might be jammed. Blain increased throttle again. More flames flashed out. As he tried to regain some altitude, the engine's rhythmic, continuous drone became an irregular stutter, and the plane began to vibrate. A glance at the revolutions-per-minute counter confirmed his fear: engine trouble. The best he could hope for now was to get his plane out of enemy-occupied territory. There was a chance.

He turned westward, pushing to maintain altitude. Any attempt to alter the carburetor mix or to clear the stuck valve failed. The acrid stench of hot metal soon overwhelmed, and the Sopwith bobbed slightly up and down in the airstream as it slowed. Blain continued to woo some effort from the engine, mile after precious mile. Then, with a frightening shriek, a piece of metal ripped through the engine cowling and flung off into the air behind them. Flames flared from the broken intake valve, and the propeller stopped dead. They were going down. The best he could do now was get himself and Griffiths on the ground alive.

When Orville Wright performed the first flight in a powered airplane on December 17, 1903, he declared it to be "the introduction into the world of an invention which would make further wars practically impossible." Wright was correct that airplanes would bring a revolution in war, but not in the way he imagined. Instead of an instrument for peace, the airplane became a multipronged weapon in a conflict that would envelope the world. The RFC was founded in April 1912 and was the forerunner to the British

Royal Air Force (RAF). They entered the war a fledgling force staffed mostly by enterprising, well-heeled amateurs. The aircraft they brought to France were made from wood, wire, and canvas; had only 70-horsepower engines; sped barely over 75 miles per hour; and took almost an hour to climb to their ceiling height of 10,000 feet. Pilots carried rifles for weapons and grenades for bombs. Soon after fighting began, however, many credited the RFC's bird's-eye role tracking troop movements with staving off the German envelopment of British troops and an early knockout blow in the war. A dispatch to London from the field commander praised the RFC's "skill, energy and perseverance."

In his pilots, Hugh Trenchard, the RFC commander in France, looked for "High spirits and resilience of youth . . . under twenty-five, and unmarried. Athletic, alert, cheerful, even happy-go-lucky, the paragon would also reveal initiative and a sense of humour. The greatest strength was an incurable optimism." Blain fit the bill.

The eldest son of a wealthy English cotton merchant, Cecil William Blain was born in 1896. As a schoolboy, he attended Loretto, a Scottish boarding school that had churned out its share of famous bankers, politicians, judges, and clergymen. The school was known for sport, and Cecil excelled at cricket, rugby, and golf. On graduation, he went to South Africa, where his uncle owned a large ranch and pineapple farm. There he tended fields, rode horses, and spent his days in the sun. The outbreak of war ended this free-spirited life. Blain felt compelled to return to

A recruiting poster to fly for Britain.

fight for his country. With his connections to the British elite, he easily secured a spot in the RFC. Its glamor and gallant reputation made it an attractive service for most young men.

He did his flight training at Northolt, London, where the instructors were mostly RFC airmen on leave from the front, some of them washed out from trauma. Crashes were frequent, often deadly. On a typical day of training, a cadet might witness a dozen. Sometimes the wreckage was so grisly the ambulance did not have to hurry. Planes pancaked on rough landings or overshot the runway altogether, smashing into trees. They overturned in the air and spiraled out of control. There were midair collisions. Engines died. Petrol ran out. Wings became untethered. Rudders stuck. Of the roughly 9,000 men who died in the RFC over the course of the war, one in four were killed in training. Blain survived, and on January 14, 1916, he was issued his wings. That June, he was assigned to the newly formed 70th Squadron, responsible for long-range patrols in enemy territory. He left for France in time for the launch of the Somme offensive.

There was nothing for Blain and Griffiths to do but land. They sailed over a French village, low enough to see its inhabitants looking up at them with incredulous faces. Blain spied a level pasture, dotted with cows, and set the plane down gently. Its wheels rumbled to a stop in the high grass, and they scrambled out. Perhaps if they were able to fix the engine they could get back up in the air. One look at the shredded crankcase dashed their hopes.

Orders were that if they should come down behind enemy lines, they were to destroy their machine so the Germans could neither use it nor learn from it. In this new battlefield in the sky, every advantage in developing technology might prove the difference between defeat or victory. The two men set upon their wooden craft, putting their fists and boots through the canvas wings. Griffiths opened the fuel tank and soaked a cloth with petrol. He circled the plane, smearing petrol across the wings, then set it on fire. Flames ran across the fuselage and wings just as German soldiers appeared, weapons drawn.

The Germans brought the two men to the nearby town of Cambrai and put them in a sliver of a cell in the old stone fortress. First they noticed the stifling heat, then the foul smell. When they tried to sleep, on two straw mattresses that filled the tiny space, they found their threadbare, soiled blankets were alive with lice. In the morning, a guard brought them some square hunks of sour black bread, their first food in twenty-four hours. Lunch and dinner were a cabbage soup that looked like filthy bathwater. It was served in slop pails.

They were let out of their cell briefly and found the prison crowded with Allied soldiers and plagued by dysentery. A wounded soldier lay on a stone floor, his upper arm a fetid gob of open flesh, dried blood, dirt, and straw. Nobody was allowed to help him. Night after night Blain lay on his mattress, too troubled to sleep. Escape crept around the edges of his thoughts, but the shock of his capture overwhelmed him.

CHAPTER 2

"There is to be a big push shortly . . . Every atom of energy must be concentrated on the task." General Hugh "Boom" Trenchard spoke in the thunderous voice—and hard-charging attitude— that had earned him his nickname. "Our bombers should make life a burden on the enemy lines . . . Reconnaissance jobs must be completed at all costs." At Le Hameau aerodrome in northern France, Captain David Gray accepted these orders with his usual aplomb. A flight leader in the 11th Squadron—home of several of the RFC's finest aces—aggression in the sky was his specialty. Trimly built, with an erect posture and a neatly pressed uniform, Gray looked military, every inch. His stern glance, accentuated by a ruler-straight part in his hair, high forehead, trim mustache, and hatchet nose, marked an officer who brooked no compromise with himself, or his command.

On September 15, 1916, after heavy artillery bombardment of the German lines that one pilot likened to a "solid grey wool carpet of shell bursts," British soldiers rose from their trenches in another major offensive on the Somme. Aided by tanks that cleared a path and provided gunfire cover, the troops overran a 9,000-yard stretch of the German trenches. Gray, his observer Leonard Helder, and scores of other RFC aircrews flew day and night, both before and after the initial ground attack. Beyond the

David Gray in RFC uniform.

threat of Archie and the risk of mechanical failure, they also faced attacks from German fighter squadrons. The RFC was increasingly being seen as a "suicide club," and a pilot who lasted a few weeks on the front was considered an "absolute master." Air crews were not issued with parachutes, and when they prepared emergency kits with rations, maps, and other gear to allow them to survive if shot down, their commanders castigated them for showing an unwillingness to fight to the bitter end.

What the crews and the British command did not yet know was that Oswald Böelcke, the fearsome German ace, was back on the Western Front. An aggressive, practiced pilot, the twenty-five-year-old Böelcke was also a keen tactical thinker. The German air force had sent him to the east for the summer, but in late August, with the RFC again holding supremacy in the sky, they ordered him back to turn the tide. Böelcke started a new squadron, the *Jagdstaffel*, whose sole purpose was to hunt British planes. He recruited the best pilots, including the young Baron Manfred von Richthofen, soon to be known as the Red Baron. Böelcke demanded that his squadron be fully supplied with the new Albatros D.III, a fast, easily handled biplane with two fixed guns. With its tactic of coordinated assault, the Jagdstaffel was a vicious force.

At their aerodromes in France, Allied pilots chronicled the rising threat in flight logs, diaries, and letters home. Mostly they tried to relax between missions. They went on walks, rode horses, drank French port, played bridge, listened to music on the gramophone, and sang songs. There was comfort in the farmhouses and châteaus where they were billeted, and they tried to forget the *wouft-wouft* of anti-artillery and the sight of friends plummeting in corkscrews to the earth, their planes on fire or split into two.

Gray reviewed his mission for September 17, 1916, pinned to the squadron noticeboard: Lead a six-plane fighter escort on a bombing run to the Marcoing rail junction to disrupt the German resupply of men and ammunition at the Somme. He suited up in preparation for the attack ahead. At 30 years of age, he was the "Old Man" in the 11th. Few, if any, had his military experience, including action under fire. His fighters, and the bomber crews they were protecting, would need every bit of it.

Gray had spent the first part of his childhood living in a tea plantation hewn out of the dense Indian jungles of upper Assam. It was a beautiful and perilous place—a land of misted rivers and dense canopies of palm trees, and also of insufferable heat, monsoons, malaria, cobras, and leopards that preyed in the dark. When he was almost eight, his family returned to England. His father opened a medical practice in London, and they lived in a townhouse in the well-heeled neighborhood of Regent's Park. The culture shock was profound, but David adapted quickly.

He settled early on an army career and attended the Royal Military Academy in Woolwich, southeast London. Founded by King George II and known as "The Shop," the academy's students were destined to be sappers—engineers who built roads and bridges and laid and cleared mines—or in the artillery. A shrill trumpet called reveille at 6:15 a.m. Then, after a parade, cadets attended lectures in the ivy-clad redbrick buildings, on everything from history and mathematics to electricity, fortifications, and explosives. They built wooden mountings for 80-ton artillery guns and soldered shell casings. They surveyed hills and dug long tunnels across the campus grounds with pickaxes and shovels.

Upon graduation, Gray was commissioned as a second lieutenant in the Royal Garrison Artillery and stationed in a fort on the Red Sea. Two years later, wishing to return to the country of his birth, he joined the 48th Pioneers of the British Indian Army. Although an infantry regiment, the Pioneers specialized in constructing bridges, fortifications, and roads in the often impassable Indian landscape. Gray was well liked both by his soldiers and by the officers above him, and he was promoted to lieutenant. His record read: "A capable and efficient officer. Good eye for country. Has tact and judgment. Energetic and self-reliant." Positions as quartermaster and adjutant followed, then a promotion to captain.

Gray also sank himself into the cultures in which he lived. Languages came to him as easily as bad habits did to others, and his nickname in India was "Munshi," teacher of tongues. Besides English, he spoke French, German, Russian, Bengali, Hindi, and Arabic, as well as a healthy smattering of several other languages.

Soon after the outbreak of World War I, the 48th Pioneers embarked from Bombay (modern-day Mumbai) with the 6th (Poona) Division of the British Indian Army. Their transport steamed up the Persian Gulf and anchored at the mouth of the Shatt al-Arab, the river created from the confluence of the Tigris and the Euphrates. The British needed to ensure a steady supply of oil from Mesopotamia for the war effort. For that, they had to maintain dominance in the region, first by wresting control of Basra from the Turks. Within days of the Pioneers' arrival, Gray led a machine-gun company in a fierce fight to take Kut-az-Zain, a fort manned by 4,500 Turks. Gray thrived in his first test of combat. The division then force-marched 30 miles across the desert to take Basra from the fleeing enemy.

In spring 1915, Allied biplanes of the newly founded Indian Royal Flying Corps soared over Basra, scouting Turkish movements in the deserts to the north. The sight inspired Gray. Here were masters of the air, flying engineered marvels able to evade or engage the enemy on their own terms. Later that year, Gray returned to London to claim a spot in the RFC flight school at Hendon. He was schooled in dogfighting by Albert Ball, Britain's most famous ace. After earning his wings in January 1916, he distinguished himself flying for a Home Defense squadron, then another in France, before the elite 11th recruited him to their fighter ranks. Soon after he became a flight leader, known in the squadron for his preternatural calm.

After a dismal breakfast in the mess hall, Gray and Helder took off in their trusted Farman Experimental FE2b. Helder was an experienced observer, and he and Gray made a fine team. Their British-built two-seater, with its V-shaped structure, stab of a tail wing, and 160-horsepower engine, had served them well on numerous missions. It carried colored streamers on the tail wing to mark it as the escort leader. Minutes after clearing the aerodrome, the engine started to knock, and Gray signaled the five other escorts to return. Ground crews prepared another FE, this one new, fresh off the factory line.

To the RFC, though, "new" meant untested and prone to fault. Gray ascended into the air again, this time without much confidence in his machine, but because of a low fog the run was postponed again, and they returned to base. At 9:30 a.m., he left Le Hameau for the third time. His friend Lionel Morris, with whom he had learned to fly, was second lead. The sky was now clear and bright. Gray and Helder circled at 10,000 feet, waiting for the arrival of the bombers. They could see the white cliffs of Dover in the distance, on the other side of the English Channel. Although it was wonderful to see their homeland, the clear skies guaranteed attack from German fighters—and the lack of clouds meant there would be no place to hide.

Helder sighted the dozen bombers from the 16th Squadron to the north: slow but sturdy BE2cs carrying 20-pound and 112-pound "eggs" under their carriages. Gray waggled his wings, indicating to the other escort pilots to tighten into a diamond formation. A red flare from the lead bomber signaled the mission was a go. With Marcoing only 35 miles away, the journey would be short. Before crossing the front, Helder fired his Lewis gun to warm up its action. No sooner had their ears stopped ringing from their own gunfire than bursts of Archie surrounded them.

An FE2b bomber and reconnaissance plane in the air during a run.

All the planes sailed unharmed through the barrage. Perhaps fortune was shining on them and the run would come off without interference. Shortly after, they spotted the sun's reflection shining from the railway track that ran to Marcoing.

The bombers were below them, at 6,000 feet, and they now zeroed in on the railway junction. Gray maintained his escort's position above, where they could prevent any diving attacks from the enemy. All his crews kept a sharp eye out. The eggs dropped one after another over Marcoing. Explosions rocked the air and sent up mushroom clouds of black smoke. Job well done by all, the 16th turned back toward the west. Gray and the other escorts turned to follow the bombers home.

Suddenly, the sky was alive with black-crossed planes swooping in from the blind of the sun. "Fritz!" Helder screamed through the rush of air. Böelcke and his Jagdstaffel drove home their surprise attack. One British bomber was ripped to pieces. Gray banked, then dove to protect the others. Watching the German planes for any change in their direction, he gauged his angle of descent to maximize his plane's arc of fire. Knees braced against the sides of the cockpit, Helder stood on his seat to better direct the Lewis gun. Its bullets cut through the air. An Albatros exploded into a ball of flame. Gray's and Helder's quick and courageous actions gave the rest of the bombers the seconds they needed to escape to the west.

The scarlet-and-black planes cartwheeled around to focus on the six escort fighters. They swarmed the British with the bewildering force and speed that would earn them their sobriquet "The Flying Circus." A close-quarter rake of bullets from Böelcke ripped through Gray's engine and shredded an aileron. Propeller stopped, balance control lost, the plane plummeted into a spin. Helder hung on to a strut to avoid being flung out. Böelcke hounded them as Gray tried to recover. Bullets punctured the petrol tank and shredded a wing. Then the German swung away to single out another fighter. The others in the Jagdstaffel swerved and sideslipped through the air in an elegant but deadly pursuit. One of them, Richthofen, aiming for his first

A dogfight on the Western Front. A British plane flies toward a falling German plane, trailing smoke on the right.

victory, chased after Morris, the second lead of the British squadron.

Ground approaching, the world a dizzying swirl of sky and black smoke, Gray fought to recover from the spin. Nothing worked. The altimeter quickly spun downward: 4,000 feet . . . 3,000 . . . 2,000. Gray wrenched the stick back and forth and pressed on the foot controls to adjust the rudder. They spiraled toward the ground as petrol sprayed from the punctured tank. 1,000 feet . . . 500 feet . . . With a sudden calm, the plane stopped its corkscrew, and they leveled out. Gray tried to restart the engine, but it was shot dead. Moments later, he crash-landed into a field crowded with German infantry and a reconnaissance balloon. His face lacerated with cuts, his arm broken, he crawled out of the plane. Helder also survived the crash. Quickly, a match was struck and touched to the wreckage. Already soaked with petrol, it burst up in flames.

Soldiers encircled the British airmen a safe distance from the blaze. A gray-haired officer approached, his Luger pistol pointed at their heads. "You are my prisoners, gentlemen," he said, in clipped English. Gray and Helder raised their arms as their plane disassembled behind them. At that moment, overhead, Richthofen put one last burst of bullets into the plane flown by Morris. It fell sideways and crashed behind some trees, 500 yards from where Gray and Helder stood. They could do nothing. Their German captor stood there, his pistol trained on them, as if confused about what to do next. "Mind if we put our hands down?" Gray asked, too much in pain, too distressed over seeing his friend go down that he did not much care about the danger his words might put him in.

Gray was quiet for the short ride to Cambrai. For a man like him, capture was a black mark of shame akin to desertion or a self-inflicted wound. He had no choice except to surrender, but that did not lessen the blow. At Cambrai, a medic set his broken arm, then soldiers hustled him and Helder through the stone fortress, down a narrow, dark stairwell to the cellars—just as they had done with Blain six weeks prior, before he was sent to the camp at Gütersloh. "The war is over for you," one said in English. Other soldiers spoke to them in German, but not once did Gray reveal that he understood them. He knew that his fluency would be an advantage only if it remained hidden. The soldiers put them into a large cell with double-tier wooden bunks. It was already occupied by several crews from the Marcoing run and also, to their great relief, two 11th Squadron officers who had not returned from their mission the day before. At least they were alive.

The following morning, waking up on a straw mattress, Gray found lice inside his shirt. Such a fastidious man, the discovery disgusted him. Later, several Jagdstaffel officers visited the British crews to gloat. Their blue-gray dress uniforms were a stark contrast to the British airmen's soiled, bloodied outfits, darkening the mood in the cell further. This was nothing compared to their despair when more RFC crews arrived, having been shot down by the Jagdstaffel.

On September 26, Gray and the others were marched out of Cambrai and boarded onto a third-class train carriage. They stopped in Douai, Valenciennes, Brussels, and Liège on their way to Germany. The battered ruins afforded them a close look at the effects of war. Everything was shrouded in a veil of gloom, the streets crowded with pale-faced widows dressed in black. At Aachen, they knew they were across the German border at last. In Cologne, they were allowed to disembark, and they sat for hours in an underground waiting room while German civilians eyed them like a horrible disease.

CHAPTER 3

Caspar Kennard's first flight in France, on October 9, 1916, was only meant to be a short one. He wanted to feel out his BE2c reconnaissance plane and to get his bearings around Saint-Omer. Air mechanic Ben Digby, whose oil-smeared face looked barely old enough to manage a beard, came with him as observer—and as his guide, since he knew the area well. Minutes after takeoff, they were already in trouble. Headed southeastward, engine rattling, Kennard could not coax the plane to climb higher than 2,000 feet. Digby turned around in the forward cockpit and signaled that they needed to circle back. They were crossing over the trenches at an altitude that put them in range of small-arms fire.

As Kennard banked around, the plane was consumed by a huge cloud. Wisps of murky white vapor blinded him, and he lost all sense of direction. Again he throttled up the engine, hoping to climb into clear skies, but the plane would not respond. Then, in an instant, they were free of the cloud only to discover themselves straight over the enemy trenches, low enough to see individual German soldiers. There was no escape. Black shell bursts surrounded them. With a terrible hiss, fragments tore through the fuel tank. One shell exploded directly under the port-side wing, tipping the plane over on its side before sending it into a nosedive.

Kennard fought to regain control. Still, they plummeted. In the frenzy, Digby was sure his pilot had been hit. He began to climb from his seat to take over the stick. Kennard waved him away. Archie boomed around the plane, followed by cracks of rifle fire from the lines. Then, with a shuddering jolt, they hit the ground. The tail of the plane almost sheared off. They bounced and careened through a field before coming to a halt. Rooted in their seats, dazed, neither Kennard nor Digby understood how they had survived the crash. In the last moment, Kennard must

World War I fighter planes in flight. The illustration is titled "The Last Loop" and the caption helpfully advises against any unnecessary "stunting" after defeating a German plane.

have righted the plane enough to avoid hitting the ground head-on, but he could not recall how he had done it.

He had only been flying solo for two dozen hours. Seven months before, Kennard had been living in the Argentine Pampas, working as a hand on a 20,000-acre ranch. It was a far cry from his homeland, Kent, England, where his father owned a large estate. Caspar spent his early years in the family's stately home, Frith Hall, outside Maidstone, and then attended Felsted School in Essex, a private boarding school. With his older brother, Keith, set to inherit the family estate, he decided to make his own way in the world and left on a steamer ship for South America. By April 1916, with newspaper accounts and letters from home chronicling the German advances at Verdun, Kennard could no longer remain on the sidelines. He returned to England and joined the RFC. Twenty-five years old, tall and big-boned, he looked like he could wrestle a steer to the ground. He had a bushy mustache and dark slicked-back hair and kept a carved wooden pipe stuck between his teeth. After earning his wings, he served in a reserve squadron before being sent to Saint-Omer. He had been there less than a week when he was shot down.

A company of German soldiers surrounded Kennard and Digby before they could climb out of the plane, and took them to a holding camp—"Somewhere behind the German lines," Kennard wrote to his parents, three days later. Although "lucky to be alive," he described being consumed by disappointment. "You can imagine how we feel. It was my first flight to the lines, and to have to come down without ever having had a decent

Caspar Kennard.

scrap of it." Days later, their captors took Digby to a camp for common soldiers and sent Kennard to an officers' camp at Gütersloh. He did not remain there for long. Hungry for more than bitter soup, bristling against his imprisonment, and desperate to be back in a fight he had only just joined, Kennard decided to attempt escape. When the guard making the lunch rounds came to his cell, Kennard hurled him against the wall, sprinted through the door, and turned the key, locking the guard in. He found himself alone in the hallway, with no plans for where to go next. If he stepped out of the building and tried to make a run for the gate in broad daylight, guards would shoot him. If he hid out until dark, he would be found missing at roll call and a search would ensue. Resigned to his mistake, he sat down and waited to be discovered.

The consequence was that the Germans delivered him straightaway to another camp, Osnabrück, where the commandant, a man called Blankenstein, had him thrown in a solitary cell, giving no indication when—or if—he would be allowed to join the general barracks. Kennard was beginning to understand that the Germans had no intention of abiding by the rules of war that should have determined his treatment. By the time he emerged from isolation, he had decided that a successful escape was his best shot of survival.

When he was led into the gravel yard for his first evening roll call, he noticed that the few straggly trees around the yard's edge looked as haunted and stark as his 28 fellow airmen who now stood, with 200 Russians and 90 French, in the cold dusk

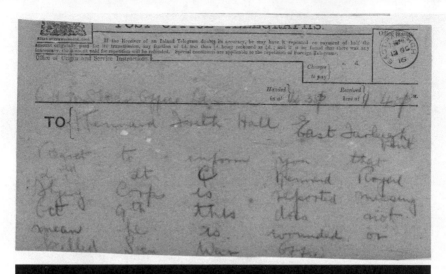

A telegram to Kennard's family informing them he's missing.

chill. Among them were Captain Gray and Second Lieutenant Blain.

Commandant Blankenstein arrived, and one of his lieutenants shouted out the roll call. Kennard answered his name when called. Otherwise he stayed apart from the other airmen, his unlit pipe stuck firmly between his lips. Once all the prisoners were accounted for, Blankenstein stepped forward and singled Kennard out in the line. Any further attempts at escape, he warned, would bring the harshest of punishments. Then he dismissed them. A guard brought Kennard to a second-floor room, where seven of his countrymen were already installed. There were beds for each of them, two chairs, a single table, and a stove—but no supply of coal.

At first, Kennard kept to himself, preoccupied with brooding over his capture and scouring Osnabrück for a means of escape.

Beyond the schedule of roll calls and meals, there was little else to do. Some of the British made friends with their fellow Russian and French officers and started language lessons. Others organized boxing and wrestling matches in the small yard. They were allowed to send two letters (of four pages maximum) and four postcards each month, so their letters home were usually written in minute script, using every inch of space. Most included requests for food, clothing, money, books, and a host of other items. The British Red Cross helped facilitate these deliveries and also sent parcels of food to British captives every two weeks. The German high command was more than happy to allow its enemy to sustain its imprisoned troops. Osnabrück also ran a brisk business out of its canteen that supplemented the meager, often putrid, meals served by the Germans. Prisoners paid for items with *Lagergeld*, specially issued camp money funded either from their military pay in captivity (per an agreement between the British and German governments) or through transfers from their own banks in England.

In early November, Kennard discovered a window with a missing latch at the end of the second-floor hallway. The window faced a 12-foot-high wall topped with barbwire. A plan fell into place.

Kennard would drop out of the window at night, cut through the fence that surrounded the barracks, get to the 12-foot wall, and climb over it onto the street below. From Osnabrück, he would take a train to a town close to the Dutch border, some 70 miles away. Once in neutral Netherlands, he would be free to return to England and to the fight. But first, he would need to learn a few words of German.

Everyone at Osnabrück knew that Captain Gray spoke German flawlessly, despite his efforts to hide it. Kennard went straight to his room and asked to be taught how to buy a train ticket in German. Gray was reluctant, especially when Kennard refused to say what preparations, if any, he had made for an escape attempt. Disciplined and uncompromising, Gray was not one to involve himself in any foolhardy ideas. Kennard revealed his plan. It was probably the most he had spoken in weeks.

Gray thought the plan had promise but suggested there was no way a few phrases in German would be enough to secure a railway ticket. Kennard would have a better chance getting to the border on foot. For that he would need a compass, food, and a map—and it would be best if he had help. With a couple men, he could gather the essentials more quickly. Together they could watch out for one another on the breakout night. Together they could support each other on the journey to the Netherlands. To round out the group, Gray recommended a third man join them. An officer called Cecil Blain had also come to him for some tutoring in German, and he had guts to spare. Before Kennard could ask, he had a breakout team. For the first time since his capture, he felt his dark mood lift.

The three men started with milk. Every school child knew that it could be used as invisible ink. Dip a fountain pen in milk, scrawl a message on a blank sheet of paper, write a note on top of that in ink, then send. The recipient runs a hot iron over the paper, and the fat in the milk below burns, revealing the hidden words—message delivered.

On the inside of an envelope addressed to his mother, Blain wrote in milk that he needed a compass smuggled in. He also wanted some warm clothes, but these could come in an ordinary package. So she would know to find a hidden message in the envelope, he put a simple code in his letter. "My dearest Mother, I am so sorry I am unable to account for the los of my letter home to you but I hop that this one will rive soon telling you that I am very fit and well. I ccannot tell you how I long to get ome again." With the additional and missing letters, the code spelled out: "Search." Gray and Kennard prepared similar messages. "Will they twig it?" Blain wondered. Even if his letter cleared the censors, he feared that his mother might not decipher the code.

While they waited, the three men acted like they were settling into Osnabrück for the long haul. They made friends with some Russian officers. At night they would have tea together and listen to concerts given by balalaika and guitar players. They even participated in a theater show with some fellow RFC pilots, twisting themselves together and acting the part of an automobile racing across the stage. The assembled men roared with laughter.

Not all was easy diversion, especially for Gray. As senior British officer at the camp, it was his job to persuade Blankenstein to provide better conditions. The floor of the latrine was like

A group of Allied POW officers at Osnabrück.

an ice-skating rink in the cold, so Gray demanded coal for its stove. He also pushed for bigger exercise grounds. Blankenstein, who turned out to be a reasonable man, acceded to both. Gray also led a protest against a spike in canteen prices. A French pilot, a man named Allouche, tried to stop it, saying the Germans were only passing off a rise in costs. Gray threatened him into silence.

Every day, Gray, Blain, and Kennard checked the parcel room for word from their mothers. At last Blain received a package from his. Closely watched by a guard, he opened the box. Inside was a handful of soft candies wrapped in wax paper and a sealed tin containing a nutcake flavored with crème de menthe. Blain thought there must have been a mistake. His mother would never have sent it—he hated mint. In the next moment, he realized what it might actually contain. He passed the tin to the guard, who shook it like a child rattling a present.

Blain remind himself to breathe so as not to give away his nervous expectation. If the guard grew suspicious, he would surely pry open the lid and look more closely. If the contraband were discovered, Blain could face time in isolation, a beating, and likely both. The guard handed the tin back and waved him away. The three men made haste to Blain's room where, sitting on his bed, Blain removed the lid of the tin. Wafts of mint rose from the sugar-coated dessert. When he lifted the cake out, he noticed that its weight was off. He dug his fingers into it and pulled out something wrapped in oilskin cloth. "Dear old Mum. God bless you," he said, hands trembling as he uncovered a compass. Overcome with thoughts of his family, how much they supported him, how much they must have missed him—and he them—tears pooled in his eyes. Gray and Kennard felt homesick too and left him to be alone.

Over the course of the week, Gray received a map, hidden at the bottom of a box of chocolates, and Kennard found a small flashlight and a file in a parcel of his own. They also collected clothes and a week's worth of tinned meat, chocolate, Oxo cubes, and milk tablets for the run to the Dutch border. But not everything they needed could come by mail. The canteen had a manicure set on sale. The Germans must not have considered how sharp it was, nor how well made: The nail clippers sliced through wire like it was paper, perfect to cut a hole in the fence. They also sewed haversacks from some canvas and made a rope out of parcel string with which to lower themselves from the window.

In early December, their preparations complete, the men were set to go but were stalled by an unexpected snowfall. No matter how dark the night, the guards would have no problem spotting their figures in the light reflected off the snow. Then a rumor started that Blankenstein knew an escape attempt was imminent. According to the prison grapevine—which the British called "The Poldhu," after the wireless station in Cornwall where Guglielmo Marconi sent the first transatlantic radio transmission—the commandant had placed six sharpshooters in the streets outside the barracks to take out anyone who managed to make it outside the wall.

At first, Gray, Blain, and Kennard did not believe it, but they kept careful watch for the next few nights and spotted some figures with rifles stalking the dark outside the walls. They decided to put the escape on hold. Surely the Germans would not maintain such vigilance throughout the long winter. Then, on December 17, Gray was informed that he was to be moved to another camp. The three were shattered by the news. Their cabal was broken.

CHAPTER 4

Two months passed at Osnabrück, and, at last, suspicion over an escape attempt abated—and the sharpshooters disappeared. On the night of February 22, 1917, Blain and Kennard slung their haversacks over their shoulders and peeked out of their room. They would have been better off with Gray still on their team, but they would have to make do. The hallway was empty. Before they could reach the broken window, they heard the whine of a door closing at the corridor's end. Someone had seen them— perhaps the French pilot Allouche whom Gray had threatened months ago, whose room was located in that direction. Even his own countrymen despised Allouche, a stickler for rules, who dressed every day with his crowd of medals on his uniform. Some even thought him a German spy.

The two men returned to their room. They would delay another day and make double-sure they were not seen. But before they awoke the next morning, six guards roused them from their beds. Commandant Blankenstein stood in the doorway as a search of the room began. The guards found their rope, their haversacks, every tool of their escape. They shoved the two Englishmen into the hallway, then down to the solitary cells in the basement. Neither of them had any doubt that Allouche had given them up. Blain was forced to remain alone in the cell for two weeks, with only plots of revenge to keep him warm. When he emerged, he found Kennard consumed by the same thoughts.

At the first roll call after their emergence, Blankenstein announced that the Germans were instituting a new policy of separating prisoners of different nationalities into different camps. Accordingly, all the British would be moved out of Osnabrück. Blain and Kennard were fine with the news—a new prison might offer better escape opportunities—but they had no intention of leaving without first exacting retribution on the "evil swine" Allouche. Several fellow British officers wanted to be involved as well. After lights-out on March 7, a dozen men tiptoed to the end of the second-floor corridor, carrying chamber pots that sloshed with the most vile concoctions of ash, urine, excrement, water, jam, and rotting food. Blain was proudest of all about his preparation: a one-pound tin of Morton's Black Treacle, courtesy of his mother. Allouche would be tasting molasses and scrubbing it from his skin for weeks. At the door, Kennard turned to the others. "Ready?"

"Not half," Blain whispered back.

They burst into the room, followed closely by the others, and pinned Allouche to his bunk, stuffing a blanket into his mouth to silence his roars. Then they poured their awful brews over him as he thrashed about with fright. At one point, Allouche freed the gag from his mouth and bellowed, *"Au secours!"* Seizing the moment, Blain dumped a fair measure of the treacle into his mouth. Revenge served, the British ran from the room. Allouche staggered down the hallway. "Help! The English have tried to murder me!" he howled. "Strike a match quickly. I am covered with blood!" Awakened by the ruckus, prisoners emerged from their rooms. One lit a match beside Allouche, and the hallway erupted in laughter at the sight of him.

The next day, Allouche pointed out the culprits to Blankenstein. When asked if they had participated in the attack, with proud smiles Blain and Kennard declared, "Yes."

Blankenstein decided to leave their punishment to the commandant at the new British camp, Clausthal. Shortly after, they assembled to go, almost a hundred men with suitcases, mandolins, gramophones, bags of food, and even pots and kettles strung over their shoulders. They aimed to leave nothing behind. A train carried them toward the snowbound Harz Mountains, 150 miles due east, deeper into Germany. Blain and Kennard watched from their carriage as they passed high into the shadowed hills. The lights in the train flickered from the jarring movement on the rails. After midnight, the train halted at Clausthal station, and the guards shouted *"Raus!"* Snow was falling as they stepped down onto the platform with their belongings. They were told they would have to wait until morning to head up to their new camp.

After a couple hours shivering in the snow, their guards allowed them into the station restaurant, where the owner spread out some ham sandwiches and hearty soup. The British bought every bottle of wine behind the bar, some of them a lovely prewar vintage. Their guards, wanting a rest too, joined them. In the temporary truce, a fine party broke out.

At first light, feeling the worse for wear, the prisoners tramped two miles into the mountains, sometimes through heavy drifts that threatened to bury them. In the distance, they sighted The Brocken, the tallest peak in northern Germany. Finally, they arrived at their new prison. Set amid mountain lakes, the building had formerly been the Kurhaus Pfauenteichen (Peacock Lake Hotel),

THE EXODUS FROM CREFELD

An illustration of Allied POWs on the move from one German camp to another.

an expansive holiday retreat. Surrounding it now was a 12-foot-tall fence made of iron-wire torpedo netting with a 2-inch mesh. Arc lights stood at intervals, so too did sentries with dogs.

Blain, Kennard, and the others who had attacked Allouche saw only the briefest glimpse inside before being shunted off to Hanover for their court-martial. They passed the night before their trial in a garrison jail, each in a lone cell with a single, iron-barred window. There were so many rats that the prisoners sounded like a percussion band as they batted the vermin away with their boots. Come morning, guards ushered them across a yard and into a courtroom. The prosecutor read out their penal-code violations for the "cunning attack" against Captain Allouche. In particular, he detailed the tarring with treacle.

A snowy Clausthal.

The French major assigned to defend the twelve accused men tried to chalk up the whole affair to a petty squabble between prisoners of different nations. The judges would have none of it. After a brief adjournment, they sentenced the lot to either pay 500 marks each or spend fifty days in solitary. Unwilling to give their enemy any funds that might be used in the war effort, the British took the time. They spent it at Clausthal in huts built behind the old hotel. Their cells grew so cold at night that the rags they were given to wash with became as stiff as boards. Never for a moment did Blain and Kennard regret their revenge.

CHAPTER 5

Captain David Gray regarded himself in the mirror. Mustache trimmed. Suit fitted. Forged pass in jacket pocket. Wallet stuffed with marks. Folded map, secret report, and some provisions in his valise. Time to go. Civilian clothes were strictly forbidden, and he had made his from a stripped-down uniform and some smuggled items. He stepped out of his room. With its warm stove, real beds, and chintz-covered walls, the Crefeld POW camp was cushy compared to Osnabrück. Holding some 800 British officers and a scattering of other nationalities, it had wide hallways, views for miles, and even tennis courts. It had been built in 1906, to house a renowned Hussar regiment, and Kaiser Wilhelm II had spared no luxury for the young German cavalrymen. Commandant Courth, a local man, was a gentle drunk who allowed his inmates to take long walks on parole in the surrounding woods.

Nevertheless, Gray was charged to escape. Partly, this was a desire to get back to the fight. Partly too, he had collected testimonies of abuse witnessed—or suffered—by his fellow officers before they arrived at Crefeld. Particularly gruesome were the reports from those in the infantry who were captured earlier in the war. His government needed to know the extent of the German crimes against his countrymen, including dreadful beatings and the cold-blooded mowing down by machine gun of those who had surrendered at the front line.

With Crefeld only 18 miles from the Dutch border, Gray knew there was a good chance he could reach the frontier—and freedom—once he got outside its high walls. Disguised as a German businessman, he intended to stroll past the guards at the double-arched front gate. His impeccable German and forged pass, stating that he had an appointment with the commandant, should do the trick. Acting like he had not a care in the world, he slowed his walk to arrive at the gate just as a truck pulled up. The guards, busy checking the driver's credentials, barely gave the suited Gray a look. In a perfect accent, he offered a few words of greeting and flashed his pass. They waved him on. With a *danke schön*, he walked straight out of the prison. He glanced sideways to see if there was any sign of pursuit or any need for alarm. He saw neither. He was just another local on the sidewalk, going about his afternoon with what leisure the war allowed. He came to a tram stop and waited for the next tram.

In the months since separating from Blain and Kennard, Gray had been carefully scouting the best way out of Crefeld. Two Russians tried to hide in a rubbish cart, but they were caught before it was taken away. Another scheme saw a dozen RFC officers building a glider plane to fly over the walls. Ultimately, it did not prove airworthy. Most escape efforts, though, were focused on tunneling under the barracks, causing the ground under Crefeld to resemble a busy ant warren. The discovery of each burrow seemed only to embolden others to try.

Commandant Courth and his guards had shown themselves effective in rooting out the honeycomb of tunnels by knocking on every wall and floor in the prison, listening for the sound of a hollow space behind. But despite his Woolwich education and experience with the 48th Pioneers, Gray did not much care for the dirty business of sapping; he wanted to try another way.

After a long wait, Gray boarded Tram 88 and paid his fare, taking one of the wooden seats hidden from the street by curtained windows. Though the drumbeat in his chest had yet to subside, he folded one leg over the other to look every bit the casual passenger. The tram delivered him to Crefeld train station, where there were trains headed due west to Venlo, the closest Dutch town. But given that he had experienced no trouble as of yet, Gray figured that he was safe to journey farther to the north, to Nordhorn, where the border might have slacker frontier guards.

He arrived at the small German textile town well after dark and left the station on foot, heading north over a series of small canals. Then he followed a road toward Neuenhaus, seven miles away. By his map, once the road intersected with a railway line, he would be a mile from the zigzagged border. A heavy rain was falling, which gave him the advantage of there not being anybody out for a late walk, but it made the going miserable. At the railway line, he turned west and started through some soggy fields. He did not have a compass, but he hoped there was little chance he would get turned around over such a short distance.

Half an hour into his hike, trousers muddy up to his knees, he reckoned he had reached the border. If there had been a demarcation, he had missed it. He took out his map. Rain pelted his face and soaked his collar. Cold, wet, and potentially lost, he dared light a match to divine his location. If a German frontier post was nearby, the guards would see the flicker of light. After several attempts to strike a match in the downpour, one remained alight long enough for him to read the squiggles of lines. He had veered a little northward in his slog, but if he made his way due south he should reach the Dutch border village of Breklenkamp.

Eventually he spotted the dim glow of a village and a wooden signpost that read "Breklenkamp." Elated, he headed down the road until he sighted an illuminated military post. A pair of soldiers in dark greatcoats sought shelter from the rain under its awning. In English, Gray explained that he was an RFC officer who had escaped from a prison camp. Saying nothing, the guards led him inside the cabin. Rising from a desk to meet Gray was a German officer, and behind him the guards seized his arms. There was not one, but two Breklenkamps, the officer explained later, separated by the border. Gray had the bad luck of having a map that only showed the Dutch town, and he had missed it by a short walk. The devastation of coming so close was profound. The next morning, they returned him to Crefeld, his secret report still hidden in his valise.

CHAPTER 6

Two hundred miles east, in Clausthal, Blain and Kennard suffered their punishment for the revenge attack on Allouche. For almost two months, the two men were in solitary confinement, inhabiting 10-by-6-foot cells between a pigsty and a mechanic's shed on the northern end of the camp. The pigs' squeals maddened them more than the tight confines and the absence of windows. At the end of May, at long last, they were allowed out. They had not bathed or exercised in weeks and had to shield their eyes from the piercing sun.

Commandant Wolfe, or "Pig Face"—as he was called by the men for his bald, round head; puffy face; and tiny, closely spaced eyes—had stripped Clausthal of everything that had once made it a tourist resort. Six officers crowded each guest room; the overflow was housed in wooden barracks. Mattresses were replaced with wooden planks and straw palliasses. Guards shook awake anybody sleeping past 7 a.m. and limited the 260 imprisoned officers to four shower heads whose pressure was little more than a trickle—they had a better chance of a wash by squeezing a damp rag over their heads. Flies infested the latrines, meals were rushed, roll calls were drawn out, and searches were frequent. Sentries and guard dogs patrolled the fence, and all parcels, including those from the Red Cross, were hacked apart to test for contraband. Still, compared to their solitary cells, Blain and Kennard thought it a palace.

The prisoners made the best of the limited grounds available to them. They laid tennis courts and imported a net at their own expense. They built a six-hole golf course, staged boxing matches, and had a theater troupe, bridge tournament, gambling den, and language lessons. When allowed out on parole, they hiked through the pine-forested hillsides under a limited guard. Some groups were content to do nothing but entertain themselves. Others passed their days reading and studying.

Blain and Kennard were a different breed—they fell into the small but distinct class of men that one veteran labeled "escape fiends." They were indefatigable.

It began with tunnels. Kennard was invited to join a breakout effort under one of the wooden barracks; then he brought Blain into the fold. The sap only needed to be 10 yards in length to reach beyond the fence, but the earth was a mix of granite and shale, and it took hours of intense digging to

YOU HAVE DER TINS—YES? NO?

Illustration of a parcels search.

go mere inches. It was tough going and also made for an awful din. During the noisiest bits, the prisoners distracted the guards by holding boisterous tennis matches. Work would have continued, but Commandant Wolfe discovered another tunnel in progress, starting underneath the stage the prisoners had built for their makeshift theater. Any further digging would have been a fool's errand.

One of the other "escape fiends," William Colquhoun, decided on a new course: straight through the wire. The Canadian lieutenant, 28 years of age and 6 foot 6 in height, had proved his mettle on the front. In early 1915, he earned the Military Cross while retrieving a mortally wounded officer under intense fire. When he was captured, a German soldier looked him up and down and asked, "Are all Canadians as tall as you?" Colquhoun responded, "Well, they call me Shorty." One day, in broad daylight, Colquhoun cut a hole in the fence around Clausthal, stepped through, and ran. Such was the brazenness of the attempt that the guards didn't notice. Some children playing in pine woods outside the camp spotted him, but the guards didn't believe them. By the time the Germans realized that he was gone, he was already far away.

A week into his 212-mile flight to the border, Colquhoun was captured by a German searching for an escaped Russian. Hours after being sent to the nearest prison camp, he busted through the skylight in his cell. He was caught again three days later by some trackers with dogs. Unbroken, he used his long arms to reach through the viewing slot in his cell door and take the key out of the lock. Although starving and exhausted, he stole a bicycle and pedaled off to the north. The bike broke, and, while trying to fix it, he was taken again. This time he was returned to Clausthal.

Blain and Kennard were just as bent on escape. They dyed some clothes black to resemble the camp workers' outfits, then forged papers using a typewriter for the text and an official stamp made with the lid of a small tin, a two-mark silver piece, and the ink from a toy printing set sold in the canteen (of all places). Then they walked straight out the gate. They only made it a few steps before the guards caught wise and hauled them back inside. Wolfe confiscated their escape kit and sentenced them to solitary once more.

It was a cruel punishment, particularly when extended for long periods of time. The isolation, the absence of physical exercise, the interminable days and nights with nothing to do but brood—all could sap a prisoner of hope or drive him mad.

As well as individual punishments of periods in solitary confinement, Wolfe made life at Clausthal collectively harder for its prisoners. Parole walks were stopped, and searches of rooms became ransacks. Some of the prisoners believed the "escape fiends" were the source of all their troubles and frowned on anyone who tried. Blain and Kennard paid no heed to these complaints, carried on through the punishments, and ignored the threat of death for even plotting an escape. They simply wanted to be free and far away from these hated Germans.

Wolfe made sure the two inveterate escape artists would not be escaping together from *his* camp. To their chagrin, the commandant removed Kennard to a different camp, breaking their partnership. Blain and Kennard were on their own.

CHAPTER 7

As the fall of 1917 neared, prisoners throughout Germany learned through the Poldhu grapevine that their captors were forming a new camp in a town called Holzminden. Expectations were high. According to the Poldhu, it was to be a "prisoner's Mecca—fine, brand-new buildings, spacious grounds, good scenery, good air." They did not know whether this was true, but the very possibility fostered great debate, both dour and hopeful.

Lieutenant Colonel Charles Rathborne looked out into the dark night of September 11, 1917, from a train headed northward from Heidelberg. Crowded into his carriage were two dozen other British officers. They passed town after town, but, except for a brief stop in Kassel, the train never slowed, thwarting a plan by several prisoners to escape by leaping from a window. They were destined for Holzminden, the first group to be sent to the new camp.

Broad-shouldered and thickset, Rathborne had soft features and a welcome smile. One likened his visage to "the face of an archbishop." Whatever his look, it belied the grit and ambition underneath. Private-school educated and fluent in German and Italian, Rathborne joined the Royal Marine Light Infantry on his eighteenth birthday. He quickly rose through the ranks, his superiors remarking that he was "keen," "energetic," and "very good in taking charge of men." In 1912, sensing that air flight was the future, he trained to become a pilot. At the outbreak of war, he was named a flight commander, then a squadron commander, then he was placed in charge of an operational wing. The mission on which he was shot down was likely one he could have sent others to perform.

As a POW, Rathborne proved no less capable. In May, he arrived at a camp in Karlsruhe, where he assumed the role of senior British officer. He fielded pleas from his fellow officers for better conditions and convinced the commandant to provide them. Escape was a high priority, but his first effort to walk straight out the gate in civilian clothes was foiled by a spy who gave away the hiding place of his escape kit. Before he could concoct a new plan, the order came for the transfer to the new camp of Holzminden.

It was after midnight when the train finally stuttered to a halt, and Rathborne and the others disembarked. In the 21 hours it had taken to travel from Karlsruhe, they had been given nothing to eat and had slept only a few halting minutes in the overpacked carriage. They dragged themselves and their few belongings a mile east to the edge of the town. At last, they arrived at the Holzminden officer camp. The former infantry barracks, built a year before the war, was ringed by tall stone walls and lit by electric arc lamps. Guards directed them through the arched main entrance on the camp's western side. Although exhausted and desperate for food, they were made to assemble in

Dublin

14ᵗʰ Feby 1886

Lieut: C. E. H. Rathborne RMLI.

H37

March 4ᵗʰ 1913

Charles Rathborne before the start of the war.

rows on the cobblestone path in front of the barracks and forced to wait in the chill of the night beneath the glare of arc lamps.

After a long time, a beetle-browed camp officer strode up, smoking a cigar. Captain Karl Niemeyer was tall and stout, like an upright rectangle. Except for his brows, his bowling ball of a head was pasty white and cleanly shaved. He wore a military cap, perched at a rakish angle. Niemeyer opened by saying that he was happy to see them, as he was "glad to see any Englishman," many of whom he called "great friends" before the war. He hoped this would be the case again, but, "in the meanwhile, war was war." He advised that they would be best served, "y'know," to write straightaway to their families and friends "for your

Holzminden.

thickest clothes, y'know. It is very cold here in winter, y'know."
He concluded, "So now, gentlemen, I expect you will be glad to
go to your bedrooms. I will wish you good-night. You will be
searched in the morning."

With that, the guards took them to the third floor of one of
the two main barracks, a four-story whitewashed building with
a mansard roof covered in slate. As they climbed the steps, many
of the prisoners still believed Holzminden might well live up to
what the Poldhu had promised. Some imagined "bedroom candles and a comforting nightcap" awaiting them. They were
divided into three rooms with high ceilings and bare walls. The
rooms had stoves, but no coal or wood to fuel them. Each officer

Karl Niemeyer.

had a small cupboard, a stool, and an iron-framed bed whose mattress was filled with straw, wood shavings, and paper. Although they were desperately hungry, the guards offered no food and the doors clanged ominously shut when they left.

Still, Rathborne and the others continued to hope for the best.

When the morning roll call was made, the 25 officers gathered outside. If they had been hungry the night before, now they were nearly faint. Beside Niemeyer stood the titular head of the camp, Habrecht. An elderly man, he had the look of a doddering old fool and merely stood by and watched as his camp officer addressed the new arrivals. Niemeyer asked if they had breakfasted. The men answered no. Niemeyer promptly ordered his guards to prepare a meal, the likes of which, he promised, "you wouldn't get in Regent Street or Piccadilly." Visions of bacon and grilled sausage overcame the British officers. They hurried to the dining hall on the second floor of their block, only to be served some tepid imitation coffee made from acorns. Nothing else. When Rathborne complained, Niemeyer pretended that he could not understand why they were upset.

As day after day passed, the officers in Holzminden were allotted little more than cabbage soup and small portions of bread. They quickly grew to despise Karl Niemeyer. A bully of the first order, he was beholden to a rash temper and a thin skin. He skulked about the camp in his starched uniform and high cavalry boots, smoking a huge cigar while seeking out trouble like a dog would a bone. No slight from a prisoner—a weak salute, a roll of the eyes, an impertinent remark—passed unnoticed or unpunished.

The prisoners did not hold back in the descriptions they recorded in their diaries and their letters home. He was a "cad," "a low-bred ruffian," "the personification of hate," "a bloated, pompous, crawling individual," "a man of unbridled ferocity and bravado," "a cheat," "a plausible rogue," and "a coward with all the attributes of one: he deceives, he is cruel, he blusters, he is dishonest, he cringes." Prone to apoplectic fits of rage, typically while brandishing a revolver or his walking cane, Niemeyer ran down and threatened prisoners with a zeal that left him red-faced and panting for breath. The root of his grievances was unclear, and, given his propensity to tell lies, his background was murky. Although born in Germany, he spent seventeen years in the United States. He might have tended bar in Milwaukee. He might have built billiard tables in New York. He might have done both. His stories changed as often as he told them. Despite being in his sixties, he claimed he had fought at the Somme—for one week, he said, which "had been enough for him."

A despicable character, Niemeyer was the perfect choice for General von Hänisch, head of the 10th Army District and responsible for overseeing POW camps in his area. He wanted Holzminden, a camp established to hold the most troublesome Allied officers in Germany, to be ruled by someone who viewed his charges as nothing better than criminals.

CHAPTER 8

Over the course of its first month in operation, officers poured into Holzminden in the hundreds, many of them inveterate escape artists from camps across Germany, including Ingolstadt, Freiburg, Augustabad, Schwarmstedt, and the dreaded underground prison Fort Zorndorf. Holzminden was in no way ready to house the hundreds of POWs and the guards who oversaw them. The cookhouse lacked dishes and had only three pots. The wash rooms had but a handful of taps and no showers. Nor was there a parcel room or a canteen from which to buy goods. If this was a prisoner's Mecca, it was a spartan one, the epitome of disorganization. There was too little food and not enough fuel to heat the stoves. Habrecht became overwhelmed. Prisoners practiced in the art of escape knew that the best chance was often in a camp's early days when chinks in its security had yet to be discovered. The chaos at Holzminden added to this opportunity.

The prison was a series of secure enclosures, one smaller than the next, like nesting dolls. On the outside was the rectangular stone wall, eight feet high and topped in places with a barbwire palisade angled at 120 degrees to prevent climbing. Within this was a half oval—like the shape of the letter *D*—protected by a 12-foot-high fence of thick mesh topped by another barbwire palisade. A chain of sentry boxes was positioned directly outside this fence. Six feet separated this enclosure from another barrier, which was the same shape and made from a simple three-strand wire fence strung on low wood posts. The space in between these two fences was no-man's-land. Prisoners were allowed only within the inner enclosure, which contained the barracks and the *Spielplatz* (a dual parade ground and exercise yard). In a sense, Holzminden was a prison within a prison within a prison, all set 150 miles from the Dutch border.

Two prisoners recently arrived from Fort Zorndorf were particularly keen to find a way out. Canadian infantry officer John Thorn, captured on the front in April 1915, had made several breakout attempts at previous camps, one of them dressed as a German war widow, black crepe veil and all. His partner was RFC pilot Wally Wilkins. Thorn and Wilkins scoured the camp for weaknesses and found a significant one. The two barracks— known as Block A and Block B—were of identical design. Each had a main building, 50 yards long, with wings at the ends that extended back and away from the Spielplatz. Each had two entrances (one at either end) facing the main grounds. Inside, stairs at both ends ran from the cellar up four floors to the low-ceilinged attic. An entire third of Block A—including the wing closest to the main gate, outside all the barriers apart from the surrounding wall—was reserved for the *Kommandantur*, the offices and sleeping quarters for the German staff. Wooden walls separated this section from the quarters of the British officers, and it had its own entrance.

Thorn and Wilkins figured that if they could open up the wooden barricade on the attic level, then they could enter the Kommandantur headquarters, come down the stairs, and exit Block A just beside the main gate. The gate was in the part of the camp occupied only by Germans, so its lone guard was unlikely to be suspicious of anybody leaving through it, especially anybody dressed in German uniform. Late at night, they snuck out of their rooms in Block A and went up to the attic. In two hours, using only a penknife, Wilkins managed to cut a small panel out of the barricade wall, which was constructed

Holzminden from the outside, its high fence and sentry boxes in clear view.

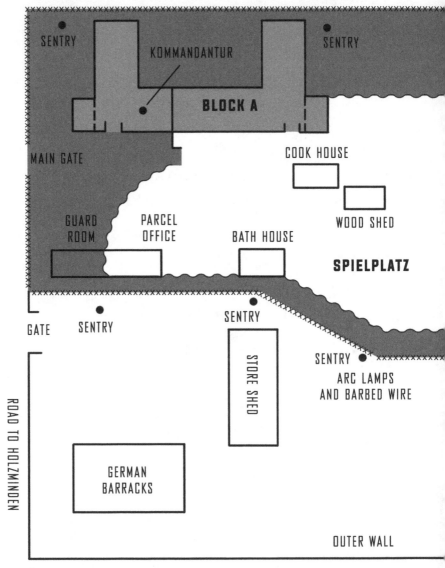

A MAP OF HOLZMINDEN

← ROAD TO HOLZMINDEN

SENTRY

KOMMANDANTUR

SENTRY

BLOCK A

MAIN GATE

COOK HOUSE

WOOD SHED

GUARD ROOM

PARCEL OFFICE

BATH HOUSE

SPIELPLATZ

GATE

SENTRY

SENTRY

SENTRY
ARC LAMPS
AND BARBED WIRE

STORE SHED

ROAD TO HOLZMINDEN

GERMAN BARRACKS

OUTER WALL

A = Medlicott and Walter's escape point
B = Block B Officers' Entrance
C = Block B Orderlies' Entrance
D = Postern gate
E = Original exit of tunnel

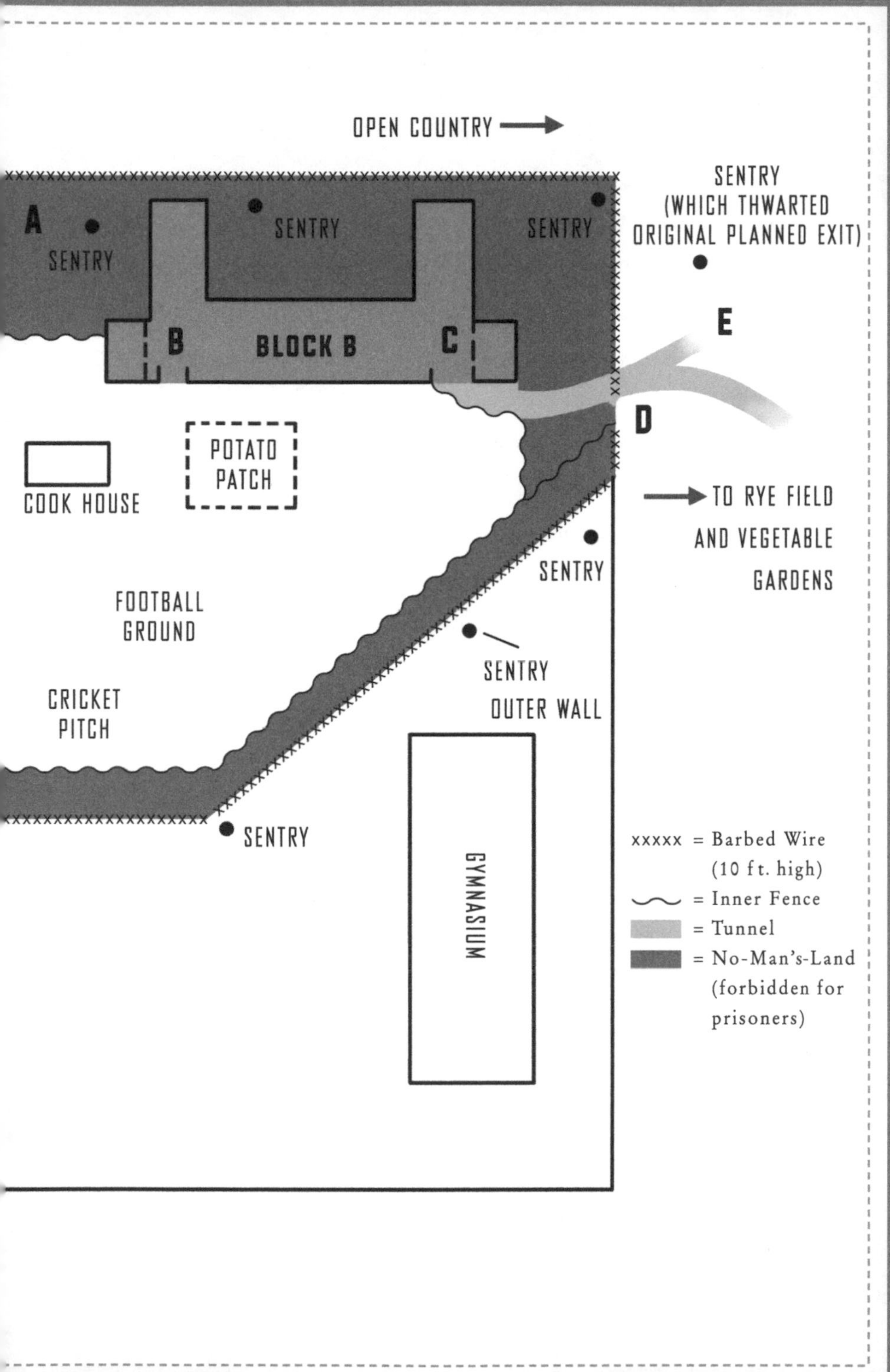

OPEN COUNTRY ⟶

A
SENTRY

SENTRY

SENTRY

SENTRY
(WHICH THWARTED
ORIGINAL PLANNED EXIT)

E

B   BLOCK B   C

D

COOK HOUSE

POTATO
PATCH

TO RYE FIELD
AND VEGETABLE
GARDENS

FOOTBALL
GROUND

SENTRY

CRICKET
PITCH

SENTRY

SENTRY

OUTER WALL

SENTRY

GYMNASIUM

xxxxx = Barbed Wire
(10 ft. high)
〜〜 = Inner Fence
    = Tunnel
    = No-Man's-Land
(forbidden for
prisoners)

from wooden planks, two inches thick and bound with wire. When they removed the panel, they found another wall of boards, thicker than the ones on their side and secured with six-inch nails bent at the ends. Wilkins was unfazed. He needed only to straighten the nails and sever their exposed ends. Then he could push the boards free. A penknife, however, would not do for the job.

Informed of the need for wire cutters, several of their friends searched the camp, and not half a day later a pair was nicked from a German soldier who was fixing the fence. After lights-out, Thorn and Wilkins returned to the attic and finished their escape hatch. A quick inspection of the German side confirmed their theory that they could access the stairs. Then they replaced the two panels, hoping they would not be discovered too soon. Next, they prepared to go. One of the prisoners had smuggled a sewing kit into Holzminden with him. Within a couple days he whipped up two jackets and two pairs of gray trousers with red stripes down the sides. Food for their border run was donated by their fellow prisoners.

On September 28, the day they were meant to go, Wilkins came down with a high fever. Knowing that the hatch might be discovered at any minute or that a new security measure might sink their plan, he gave his place to Reginald Gaskell, a British Indian Army captain and fellow veteran of Fort Zorndorf. After answering to their names at the last roll call of the day, Thorn and Gaskell returned to the barracks, donned their disguises, and placed their civilian clothes and knapsacks into two of the plain sacks the guards often used during work detail. An hour later, they crawled through the barricade wall in the attic, replaced the panels behind them, and descended the stairs into the Kommandantur. Just before they got to the door, they saw Habrecht and several other Germans. They continued on, not saying a word. Nobody stopped them. Once outside, they made a beeline for the main gate and did not slow down until they had passed the guard and were out and away.

The next morning roll call came, and still there had not been an alarm. When a guard called the names of Thorn and Gaskell, their fellow prisoners answered for them. Then Niemeyer arrived onto the Spielplatz and summoned Thorn—something to do with contraband found on him when he first arrived at Holzminden. Not wishing to risk further subterfuge, a British officer who had helped prepare the escape stood forward. In a calm voice, he announced that Thorn "had left the evening before on a journey to Holland." A great cheer rose among the prisoners, sending Niemeyer into a steam. He demanded the roll call again, and Thorn and Gaskell were found missing.

Commandant Habrecht, a man predisposed to inaction, left the matter for Niemeyer to handle. He ordered everyone to return to the barracks, and a search began for how the two officers had escaped. Bloodhounds were brought in. Freshly arrived from Clausthal, "Shorty" Colquhoun shared a room with Thorn. Thinking quickly, Colquhoun sprinkled cayenne pepper into his fellow Canadian's old shoes. Then he took Thorn's socks and replaced them with his own. The same was done for Gaskell. Soon enough, the guards gathered up the escapees' remaining clothes and shoes and brought them out onto the Spielplatz. The bloodhounds first took the scent of the socks and began racing around the camp like they were chasing ghosts. Watching from the windows, Colquhoun and the others could barely contain their laughter. Then the dogs buried their noses in the boots laden with pepper. After a good whiff, they went completely mad, leaping about, hurling themselves back and forth, their handlers barely able to keep a grip on their leashes. Shouts and hollers followed from the windows. Enraged by the scene, Niemeyer drew his revolver and brandished it at the barracks.

After an intensive inspection, which failed to uncover the hatch, the Germans had no idea how Thorn and Gaskell got out undetected. A drain, sniffed out by the dogs, was suspected as a possible route until its diameter was determined too small to fit a man. Still, it was cemented closed. Wilkins, who was by now feeling better, decided to use the attic hatch for himself the following night. Others aimed to follow. For all its rings of defenses, perhaps Holzminden was not the unbreakable fortress that Niemeyer boasted.

Then on October 1, 1917, Holzminden was visited by General Karl von Hänisch of the 10th Army Corp Division, an ogre of a Prussian officer and Habrecht and Niemeyer's superior. The

Poldhu relayed that Hänisch's son had been killed by the British, and it was clear he hated them. The prisoners, now numbering over 500, paraded into the Spielplatz and drew together in straight lines, under the close watch of Niemeyer. They showed proper form and answered their names promptly when called. They had only just started to receive food parcels to supplement their diet, and they intended to give the general no reason to stop deliveries or to make their lives any more difficult.

All the staff, from Commandant Habrecht down, were present, dressed in their finest uniforms, their boots polished to a

General Karl von Hänisch, head of the German Army 10th District.

shine. The previous night another handful of prisoners had got away, their method unknown, and Niemeyer intended to use the escapes to get himself promoted over his superior. General Hänisch was quiet throughout the roll call, but as he toured the barracks and other facilities he made no secret of his feelings toward the prisoners. They were "barbarians" and "*schweinhunds*," and, in his opinion, "they did not deserve to be allowed to live, let alone receive letters." Niemeyer agreed. No treatment was too harsh for their enemy.

Near the end of his short visit, Hänisch allowed Major John Wyndham, the senior British officer, to address him. Forty-six years old, an army lifer and veteran of several campaigns, Wyndham was unafraid. In German, he first demanded better accommodation for his men. "There are no public rooms, no library, one solitary cookhouse, and no bathroom," he said. Hänisch turned to Habrecht and Niemeyer. They spoke quietly, then the general responded that a proper bathroom and another cookhouse would be provided. The rest were luxuries.

Back in his office, Habrecht gently suggested to Hänisch that the British major, and the prisoners overall, deserved some modicum of respect. Niemeyer interjected that respect was something they were given too much of. Within 48 hours of the general's departure, Habrecht was ordered to pack up his office. Niemeyer was now completely in charge.

As some of his first acts as commandant, Niemeyer ordered a guard to fire at prisoners in the barracks building who were mocking the Germans during their morning drill marches. He made the sick and invalid stand in the parade ground for hours in the cold. He shut all the prisoners in their barracks for a day. And he ordered that any officer caught in the act of a breakout be shot on sight.

Still, the escapes continued.

Throughout October 1917, batches of prisoners continued to arrive at Holzminden, many among them with a roster of failed escapes under their belt. Over sixty men came from Ströhen, including David Gray and Caspar Kennard, who had found themselves together there again after being shuffled from camp to camp. The new prisoners gathered in the Spielplatz, its grass now trampled into a muddy soup because of the rain and daily tread of hundreds of boots. Prisoners stood on one side, guards on the other, then Karl Niemeyer performed his typical routine for newcomers. The Ströhen arrivals knew Niemeyer well—he had been the camp officer there before Holzminden was opened and had ordered guards to bayonet prisoners. Three of them had been seriously wounded. When asked to account for his order, he had declared, "I had nothing to do with it all. I was not in the camp. I did not give the order."

"Look at these criminals and mark them down," Commandant Niemeyer said to his guards. "These are not officers and gentlemen, they are criminals, and I hope you will treat them such."

One officer bluntly said, "Oh shut up, Niemeyer."

Niemeyer flushed. "Did you tell me to shut up?"

"Yes I did," the officer said.

A POW's humorous illustration of Niemeyer.

"Then I'll have you arrested immediately. In five minutes!" Niemeyer roared.

Some of the officers snickered at his lack of certainty, some a little too loudly. Niemeyer ordered the guards to clear the Spielplatz. "You are very clever? Yes? Well, I make a special study of this escaping. You will not escape from here. You think I, the commandant, know nothing. You are wrong. I know damn all." Paroxysms of laughter followed his mistaken admission of being a know-nothing.

The prisoners were hurried at the point of bayonets to their assigned barracks. There they quickly learned about the removable panel in the attic. Despite intensive searches, more sentry patrols, widening the stretch of no-man's-land, and interrogating anyone who had escaped and been caught on the run, Niemeyer had yet to discover their method. More than a dozen prisoners had used the hatch, and there was a veritable German-uniform factory in one of the barracks rooms.

However, not a single man had yet succeeded in making the long journey to Holland. Thorn, Wilkins, Gaskell, and all the others were captured on their runs to the Dutch border. It was risk enough to escape the walls of Holzminden, but that was only the first step to freedom.

CHAPTER 9

"Get up!" A guard pounded on the door, rousing Gray and the three other officers with whom he shared a room in Block B. The pounding, and the call, were repeated down the corridor. If they did not rise quickly enough, guards would enter their cells and shove them out of bed with the butts of their rifles. Roll call was at 9 a.m. sharp, and the prisoners spilled out of the barracks onto the snow-dusted Spielplatz to make it. Stragglers and those who failed to properly salute—or to stand at attention in uniform—were rewarded with a stay in the jug for a day, or three. "Cost price," Niemeyer would say in his shaky grasp of American idiom. No matter how cold the day, the men were forced to wait an interminable time as one of Niemeyer's lieutenants walked up and down the lines, calling out names and checking them off his list.

Since arriving at Holzminden, Gray had realized that Niemeyer had created an environment intended to dehumanize the officers by a thousand petty humiliations. Apart from the dining room, which could only seat a hundred men at a time, there were no common rooms in which they could assemble. This meant that most prisoners ate where they slept. The officers conducted church services at the ends of corridors or in stairwells, where gatherings for lectures and card games were also held. Men scrambled over and around one another like ants in a nest. One was almost never alone with one's own thoughts.

Waiting was one of the most subtle instruments of harassment used. They waited for morning roll call, and when it was over, they waited for a wash at the taps in the yard. They waited for a paltry breakfast of bitter coffee and hard biscuits. They waited to get close enough to the noticeboard to see if they had a new parcel. If they did, they joined another line and waited to receive the parcel, then they waited again while the guards hacked to pieces or spilled out onto the table items their family or friends had sent. The queue for parcels started in the morning, and if you were not there early enough, you could well be waiting until the end of the day.

They waited to use a stove, of which there were too few, to cook their lunch. They waited for yet another round of inoculations.

The dining room at Holzminden.

The cookhouse at Holzminden.

They waited to use the lavatory. To buy firewood at the canteen. To get their ration book for bread and wine. They waited for letters that did not come. For their name to be called at the 4 p.m. roll call. For whatever watery stew they were serving for dinner. Once a whole cow's skull was found floating in the cauldron they dished it from. By 6 p.m., when they were locked in for the night, they had spent hours standing, waiting, time stretched out to lengths they never could have imagined.

The little tyrannies exercised on the prisoners at Holzminden were almost limitless. Despite—or perhaps because of—the inviting countryside outside the walls, Niemeyer refused to grant parole walks. As a result, they had only the half oval of

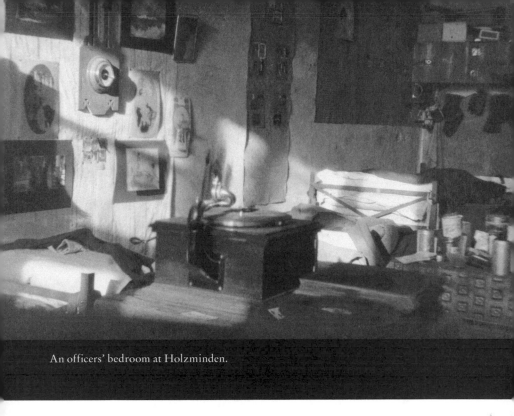

An officers' bedroom at Holzminden.

grounds inside the wire for exercise and recreation. This was at best 410 yards around, space taken up by two cookhouses, horse troughs, a woodshed, a parcel office, a potato patch, and a dozen straggling trees. They tried to create a cricket pitch and football field in this limited space, but Niemeyer prohibited most games, telling them that one of the arc lamps had been broken by an errant ball. Their offer to pay for its replacement was met with silence. There was a gymnasium, built for the original barracks, but it was set between the inner wire and the surrounding walls—out of bounds. And so, when not in line or sitting in their packed rooms, prisoners wandered back and forth in the crowded Spielplatz like penned cattle.

Bathing facilities were a horse trough that had hot water only twice a week, and the men had to wash in full view of the rest of the camp. A shower block was built on the senior officer's request, but Niemeyer decided to use it to shelter his Alsatian guard dogs instead. He even posted a sign outside: "When a more suitable place in the camp can be found for the dogs, officers may have baths on Tuesdays and Fridays."

Theft was pervasive. The guards destroyed the cakes, bread, meat, and other food sent to the prisoners with shameless glee, but they also stole what they pleased, especially cigarettes and soap. Letters from home, often describing what had been sent, were "misplaced." Goods were supposed to be sold at cost, but prisoners were charged triple the prices of other camps on everything from coffee, wine, butter, firewood, eyeglasses, pencils, razors, notepads, watches, and toilet paper. Niemeyer also extorted charges for such necessities as food, hot water, and fuel for the kitchens. As well as turning a blind eye to outright theft, he also set the tone of abuse at the camp—and reveled in it. He paraded about the camp grounds and barracks throughout the day, hands stuffed in his greatcoat, chewing on his cigar. His voice could change from a soft dolorous coo at one moment to a harsh rasp the next. He spat on the floors in front of the British officers. He ordered rooms emptied at bayonet point and conducted searches that left beds and lockers in shambles. For no reason other than a sour mood, he sent men to solitary or closed the parcel room.

The nonstop pinpricks that came with Niemeyer's rule left the men feeling rattled and helpless. One officer at Holzminden wrote to his mother, "Time drags slowly on here, much the same day after day; it is extraordinary how restless one gets after a while—you feel that you must be doing something, yet cannot settle down to anything." Some had lost a great deal of weight, others went listless, and one or two were spiraling into madness. With winter coming, and very little fuel to heat their rooms, their lives were certain to get worse.

"The wearisome sameness of the days, the monotony of the faces, the unchanged landscape, the intolerable talk about the war, all these tended to produce the effect of complete and utter depression," one prisoner wrote. "This was far and away our worst enemy: whole days were drenched in incurable melancholia." Second Lieutenant William Harvey likened the effect of barbwire disease to a green mold that grew thick on his mind, leaving him stale and incapable of joy.

There was no outlet to air their grievances. Niemeyer refused to meet with Wyndham and the other senior officers, nor would they have had much luck with him if he had. As far as he was concerned, his countrymen were the ones suffering because of the British and their allies. A rumor circulated the camp that Germany and Britain had met in The Hague to review POW and civilian internment conditions. From what they could make out, officers from both countries who had been held for more than 18 months would soon be sent to neutral Holland and Switzerland, where they would remain until the end of the war. But the war showed little sign of ending, and internment in Holland seemed a fool's promise.

Each man would have to find a way to survive the place they now called "Hellminden" or the "Black Hole of Germany."

Some of the men remained determined to survive it by escaping. In late October, several officers, including Kennard, made a break through the as-yet-undiscovered panel in Block A. Kennard ran into trouble attempting to cross the river Weser, whose width and fast current made for a perilous swim. He was caught, returned, and sentenced to a solitary cell. He was one of the last to use the hatch. After yet another intensive search, the guards found it at last, and a whole new series of security measures was put in place. The barricades in Block A were reinforced with iron sheets. Permit passes were instituted for the main gate and elsewhere. Windows were nailed shut. Barbwire fences were raised. The censoring of letters and inspections of parcels intensified. The barracks were scoured for contraband, and the number of guards increased. Niemeyer made every effort to ensure that the black mark on his record from all those early escapes would be erased by the prevention of any future ones. The Holzminden inmates were clearly jailbreakers of the first order, and not only did he intend to make the prison impervious to their schemes, he would crush their spirits while he was at it. "You see, gentleman," he announced to the whole camp, "you cannot get out now. I should not try; it will be bad for your health."

Private Dick Cash of the 19th Battalion, Australian Imperial Force, had no plans to escape. Cash was one of Holzminden's 130 orderlies, and, while the camp was a terrible place, his chances of starving there or being worked to death were slim compared to the salt mines or forced-labor camps that his rank could be subject to. When war broke out, Cash was 37 years old, a father of three and owner of a small grocery store and photography business in Thirlmere, Australia. He arrived on the front in March 1917, and his battalion saw its share of heavy fighting. On May 3, they were ordered across no-man's-land in an early morning assault on the strategic German stronghold at Bullecourt. The Australians faced withering heavy machine-gun fire in their approach to the enemy lines.

The POW officers at Holzminden.

During the attack, Cash was shot in the chest. The bullet punctured his left lung, but he continued ahead. A series of mortars threw him first skyward, then sideways. Shrapnel pierced his back, and many of his teeth were knocked out before he landed in a shell hole, boots first. The ongoing barrage then filled up the hole around him until all but his head was underground. There he remained for almost 30 hours, trying to squirm his way free, before he was taken prisoner. Field surgery and a torturous 300-mile ride into Germany had followed. Cash managed to survive the maggot-infested squalor and rough attention accorded many wounded Allied prisoners and spent the next couple months at a hospital in Hamelin. By September, he had recovered enough to work as an orderly. Compared to the horrors he had faced on the front and in hospital, Cash knew that he could abide Holzminden for as long as he had to in order to survive and get back to his wife and family.

He lived with the rest of the orderlies, many of whom were also recovering wounded, in Block B. Twenty men slept in the same size room as 12 officers, who were already tightly quartered at that number. The orderlies got out of their cold beds before the officers woke up. They dressed in gray-blue tunics, trousers, and caps sewn with bands of yellow cloth down the sides, and their prison number stamped in red on the front of their shirts. On the back, in large letters, was KG (*Kriegsgefangener*—prisoner of war). At 7 a.m., they began their day serving as the "nanny" or "batman" for five officers. They steeped pots of tea. They collected their uniforms, caps,

Barracks Block B.

and boots and polished and cleaned them before the wake-up call. Then they ate their own breakfasts before showing up for morning roll call. After that, they returned to their officers' rooms to make their beds, empty their ashtrays, and tidy up. Then they swept the corridors and staircases. Twice weekly, they changed the bedsheets and beat the rugs of dust.

The Germans then typically assigned the orderlies to some menial task around the camp such as bundling up paper or hauling firewood. After that was complete, they returned to their officers' rooms to straighten up, make tea, and help serve meals. Most of the work was fairly light, albeit monotonous, and they rotated rooms so they did not have to suffer any particularly needy officer for long. As one orderly wrote, "Taking the officers by and large, they were a pleasant and easy going crowd, perhaps inclined to be a little thoughtless." For those "tartars," the orderlies could always exact a trivial retribution—a broken teacup, undercooked food—to signal that they could only be pushed so far.

None of this service seemed odd to Cash, his fellow common-rank soldiers, or the officers they served. Although they were all prisoners, so traditional was the class separation between them that not even Niemeyer, who abused them all at every opportunity, ventured to make the officers fend entirely for themselves. European society had a rigid class system, and the military was yet another beast. However, officers and orderlies alike knew that they were all in this war together. They all faced the cruelties and whims of Niemeyer, the dreary repetition of days, the interminable lines, the thefts, the meager amounts of food, and most important of all, the absence of freedom.

A number of orderlies had helped officers escape from other camps, providing them with uniforms and acting as lookouts. They intended to do the same at Holzminden. Dick Cash, with his toothless smile, made clear to the top breakout artists his willingness to help.

CHAPTER 10

Shorty Colquhoun wanted to dig a tunnel. Since the Germans' discovery of the escape hatch, he could see no other way out. Although the tunnels British prisoners had started at other camps had fallen shy of success, he remained confident that one could be pulled off at Holzminden. Desperation often steeled the spine that way.

Finding the best place to start a sap would be a simple exercise in eliminating options. Given the number of Germans inhabiting Block A, Colquhoun crossed that off the list of options straightaway. The cookhouses and woodshed in the Spielplatz were easy to access but were too public and too far away from the surrounding camp wall. So that was another possibility eliminated. That left Block B. Most of the cellar space underneath the officer's section contained detention cells, and guards watched over the corridor night and day. The cellars under the orderlies' quarters in Block B, which were used to store wood, tins, bread, potatoes, and other goods, were the only other option. Although guards did patrol there, they did so infrequently. Further in their favor was the cellars' location adjacent to Holzminden's eastern wall. A tunnel would only need to stretch some 15 yards to reach beyond the camp wall—out into an unguarded field.

Colquhoun wanted to get down there to see whether a tunnel was possible. The officers and orderlies each had their own entrance to the barracks: the officers' in the west wing; the orderlies' in the east. Officers were forbidden to use the orderlies' entrance, and a guard posted 12 yards opposite the door watched all comers and goers. But nobody registered when orderlies entered the officers' section to carry out their daily duties. There, Colquhoun saw his opportunity. He recruited his friend William Baxter Ellis, a young RFC pilot, to join him on the reconnaissance. Orderlies provided uniforms and a duplicate key for the cellar door. During lunch, when most of the Germans were inside the Kommandantur, the two men crossed the yard and entered the eastern wing. Even though Colquhoun was tall and gangly, nobody paid him—nor Ellis—any mind. Inside, they found that the layout was a mirror image of their own wing.

They could either take the short flight of concrete steps up to the ground floor, or the ten steps to their right, down to the cellar. They went down. Before they arrived at the locked cellar door, something caught their attention. The Germans had walled off the space underneath the steps with six-inch wooden planks. A quick rap on them revealed the space behind the wall to be hollow, and they guessed it was there to prevent anyone lying in wait to jump an unsuspecting guard. They both realized that the space might well present the perfect opportunity: It gave them access to the cellar floor and walls, it was out of sight, and it was out of the way of the normal foot traffic of the guards. Starting a tunnel in one of the cellars would have risked discovery. If they could create a secret door in the planks, Colquhoun was sure, they had a very good chance of keeping their activities secret. But if the edge of the door was in any way obvious, the Germans were sure to find it.

"Will you join our tunnel effort?" That was the question on Colquhoun and Ellis's lips. The answer was a definite yes from David Gray. It was the best chance of escaping Holzminden. The answer was also an easy yes for infantry captains Joseph Rogers (a former coal-mine engineer) and Frank Moysey. They had been involved in tunnel attempts at all their previous prisons, where they had built sliding steps and hinged walls to disguise access. They nicknamed their band of tunnelers the "Pink Toes," likely due to the state of their feet after hours burrowing through the frigid ground.

In comparison to some of those projects, this new tunnel was a small matter. First, they would need carpenter's tools, and for those they would need a carpenter. They smashed in a door in their quarters, making sure to knock it off its frame and mangle the lock—something only an experienced tradesman could fix. One such arrived later that day, his box of tools in his hand. A guard was there to watch over him while he worked. Next, the distraction. Colquhoun and his coconspirators, including Gray, launched into an argument with the guard—some minor disgruntlement. There was a lot of shouting, and a few of the officers staged a scuffle with each other. While the carpenter watched the affray, one of the officers slipped behind him and nicked almost everything apart from the toolbox itself, including a fine-toothed, thin-bladed saw. After the melee had ended and the officers cleared away, they waited to see if there would be a search for the missing tools. What they suspected, and hoped, was that the carpenter, and the guard responsible for him, would not admit to anybody that they had been foolish enough to fall for the deception. Their suspicion proved well founded.

The next day, disguised in borrowed yellow-banded tunics, Moysey and Rogers ventured through the eastern entrance of Block B, accompanied by a real orderly who was there to keep lookout. A quick examination of the walled partition showed that the best place to create a door was near the bottom of the steps where the planks were longest. At the top of the last plank, there was a small opening from some badly fitting boards where a slide bolt could be hidden. Reaching it would be a tight fit for even the most slender of fingers, but possible.

Moysey and Rogers were quick to the task. They unscrewed the whole V-shaped panel from its placement. An inspection of the chamber behind confirmed exactly what Colquhoun had hoped: It gave access to the floor as well as to the main, load-bearing walls on the eastern and southern sides of the building, and it was almost tall enough to stand up in. Measuring five yards long and four yards wide, it was also big enough to pack the excavated soil and rubble for a 15-yard tunnel, which eliminated the need to smuggle it out for dumping. They cut a three-plank door out of the partition wall and then reattached it with two hinges. Such was their precision that there was almost no visible seam between the 18-inch-wide door and the wall.

Door panel pivoted here

Illustration of a secret panel made in a door by World War I escapees, using similar techniques as the Holzminden men.

They also mounted a bolt on the door, its latch just within reach behind the wall. After sweeping the sawdust into their secret chamber, they replaced the whole panel and secured the bolt. So snug was the fit they could barely spot the door themselves. Tools hidden under their tunics, they walked back up the steps and out into the Spielplatz.

The tunnelers wasted no time and launched immediately into the digging. Colquhoun and Ellis had the honor of going first. Once inside the chamber, they removed the bricks on the southern wall, then dug into the concrete with a chisel. After a few inches, they hit some reinforced iron rods. Even the sharpest of hacksaws would be challenged by the iron. They took the obstacle in their stride. What they needed was sulfuric acid, to burn through the iron like a flame into paper. They could not exactly buy a vial of sulfuric acid in the canteen, and obtaining some via a coded message to friends or family in England would take too long—if they managed to avoid its interception. Outside help was required.

They wanted their cabal small, twelve officers at most, to keep the tunnel secret and to avoid having too many different faces going in and out of the building. The solution, they decided, was to ask more orderlies for help. They would not need to know their purpose, except for a select few. Given that the orderlies had greater ability to move around the camp than the officers, they might be able to obtain any special items needed. Willing accomplices were soon found. One of them happened to know a civilian workman at Holzminden who could obtain some sulfuric acid. A bribe of 50 marks was the price of his conscience.

On November 5, without explanation or warning, several of the most senior and outspoken prisoners were removed from Holzminden, including Major Wyndham, Lieutenant Colonel Rathborne, and Captain Gray. Throughout the day, and into the next, Holzminden received what one prisoner labeled an "eye-wash." Officers and orderlies alike were instructed to straighten their rooms and barracks. The bathhouse was opened for use, burned-out electrical bulbs were replaced, windows were opened, walls were given a fresh coat of paint, and fuel was supplied to heat their rooms. The next day, they discovered the reason: a "surprise" visit from Dr. Rudolf Römer, the Dutch attaché assigned to inspect German camps for compliance with the Hague Convention.

The men tried to air their unjust treatment, even in the presence of the camp commandant, but Niemeyer always had an answer. On the poor quality of the food: This was simply a matter of "taste"; anyway, the men had their "private supplies." On charging for boiling water: The men were not "compelled to pay this sum." On the exorbitant prices at the canteen: "Most of the articles were sold at a loss." On the excessive stays in solitary, including those suffered by Kennard and others who had escaped from the attic hatch: The accused needed to be secured before their court-martial; only after that did the new 14-day punishment limit come into effect. On the lack of recreation space: This could be created out of sleeping space, but then the displaced men would further crowd the other rooms. On the long lines to obtain parcels or food tins: The prisoners simply showed a "lack of enterprise."

The whole inspection was a charade. When Römer's report was released, it stated that there was little cause for concern. The officers' complaints were minor in nature and "could be obviated with a little mutual goodwill." After chronicling the need for some slight improvements in the exercise grounds and sleeping arrangements, he concluded, "The general impression that I was able to gather was of a favourable nature. All the officers looked well and appeared to be in good spirits . . . The Commandant, although maintaining strict discipline, appeared desirous of doing everything possible to render the life of the prisoners as bearable as circumstances could permit."

In London, Lord Newton, head of the Prisoner of War Department at Downing Street, doubted the official report. He had received troubling secret intelligence about Römer from contacts in the Foreign Office. Informants suspected that he had compromising connections with German high officials, and, according to Römer's former colleagues, he was "professionally incapable," "amenable to bribery," and "a pathological liar." He had issued similarly positive reports of other camps controlled by Hänisch that were contradicted by a binder full of interviews from escaped prisoners. Similar testimonies were now coming in to London about Holzminden, one by an RFC captain who smuggled a coded letter out of the camp. He recounted a string of brutalities, including one occasion when four guards cleared his room to make way for newly arrived prisoners. "The first officer was seized by the throat and shaken; the second was struck with a rifle, and the third chased down the passage, his pursuer jabbing at him with his bayonet." Other prisoners, who had been sent away from Holzminden only to escape from their next camp, recounted much the same. One said that Hänisch ran his camps with "organized malevolence." Another that "Holzminden was an inferno."

Lord Newton had tried the diplomatic route, submitting letters and complaints. These had little effect. He also sat down with the Germans and negotiated to improve conditions. In summer 1917, both parties had signed up to reduce punishment lengths and to begin exchanging some prisoners, but Newton's faith in this process had been challenged by reports that the

Germans were continuing indefinite detentions and had only just begun sending POWs to internment—and in limited numbers at that. The other tool available to Lord Newton was instituting reprisals against German POWs until things got better for the British. But this only provoked countermeasures by the enemy, a tit-for-tat "special treatment" that worsened conditions for all.

CHAPTER 11

There was never enough food at Holzminden, and some of the men were suffering from malnutrition because their diet relied almost exclusively on tinned food. There was scarce fuel for the stoves too, leaving the barracks frigid. Many had already stripped their rooms of any available wood to burn—bedboards, locker doors, even furniture. Niemeyer continued to harass them at every turn. He opened and closed the bathhouse and the parcel room on a whim. He promised the new senior British officer that he would reopen negotiations around parole walks only to rescind the promise soon afterward. He offered to allow concerts and theatricals only to cancel them before the performance. In response, some acted out little revenges. They crafted an effigy and dangled it from an attic-floor window, a noose around its neck. Niemeyer went berserk, firing at the dummy as the prisoners bobbed it up and down, shattering the glass in several windows. Another officer dumped a sack of potatoes from a window as Niemeyer passed underneath. The greatest revenge of all, they knew, would be to escape.

Gray was returned to Holzminden from Ströhen in mid-December, and he went straight back to work with the Pink Toes on the tunnel. On one of his first days back, he met two officers at 11 a.m. in Room 24, on the ground floor of Block B's officers'

Kennard, gaunt from lack of food and malnutrition at Holzminden.

quarters. From under a false bottom in a wooden box they took out orderly uniforms and dressed. They smudged their faces with dirt, the better to look like common-rank prisoners who had just finished a work detail. Then they waited to get the call from the lookouts. One orderly stood watch at the entrance to his quarters, making sure there were no guards lingering in the stairwell or cellars. Once he counted the last guard to leave for his midday meal, he walked onto the Spielplatz and scratched the top of his head. Colquhoun, who was loitering outside the officer entrance, ostensibly reading a book, received the signal. He glanced toward the Kommandantur to ensure no guard was coming out. Seeing no one, he hurried inside and straight to Room 24. "All clear," he said. With that, Gray and the two others put on their black caps banded in yellow, stuffed some struts of wood under their shirts, and emerged from Block B.

Other officers in their cabal kept a keen eye on the guard stationed in no-man's-land, 12 yards opposite the orderly door. If he made a sudden movement, or gave any indication of recognizing the orderlies were in fact officers, he was to be approached and distracted in conversation. The tunnelers figured this was unlikely. There were roughly two platoons of 30 guards each that patrolled the camp grounds. They rotated beats and hourly shifts frequently to maintain sharpness, a routine that resulted in the same guard occupying the same spot only once every other week. With 550 officers and 100 orderlies, the chances of a guard detecting an unusual face entering the orderly quarters was minimal.

Gray and his digging partners arrived at the orderlies' door without trouble. On closing it behind them, they waited for another lookout to confirm that all was still clear. Only then did they move down the steps. At the panel wall, they were met by another orderly. He reached into a thin hole at the top of the secret door and unlatched the bolt. The thin door swung open, and the three officers stepped sideways into the dark chamber. The orderly closed and bolted the door behind them. He would return in two and a half hours so the officers could return to their quarters, change, and be nearby for the afternoon roll call.

Slivers of light between the planks were all that illuminated the space until Gray struck his lighter and the shadows of the three men danced upon the low walls. After unburdening themselves of the wooden struts they had smuggled inside their shirts, they lit a few lamps. These were made from empty shaving-cream tins, with holes punched through the top from which extended wicks made from twisted cloth soaked in alcohol. They could now see well enough to change out of the orderly uniforms into the plain work outfits they would wear while digging. For Gray, these damp, streaked clothes used by all the tunnelers were anathema, as even in captivity he kept himself spotless and his shirt and pants pressed to sharp creases. The clothes smelled too, as did the whole chamber—a mix of mud, rot, sweat, dead mice, and stale air. Nevertheless, stifling his disgust, Gray put on the outfit.

By now, Colquhoun and the other Pink Toes had burned through the iron rods in the southern foundation wall—just up from the cellar floor—by pouring sulfuric acid against them from clay cups. From there, they had started the tunnel proper. Using spoons and the legs of their iron bedsteads, they created an oval sap, almost one and a half feet in diameter. At first, they extended the tunnel three yards straight out from underneath the orderly entrance. The depth was minimal, and the men could hear the voices of those walking above. Then they veered the sap sharply to the left (eastward) toward the camp wall. To increase its depth, they dug at a 45-degree downward slope for roughly six yards before leveling out.

A CROSS-SECTION OF THE WORKING AREA AND ENTRANCE TO THE TUNNEL

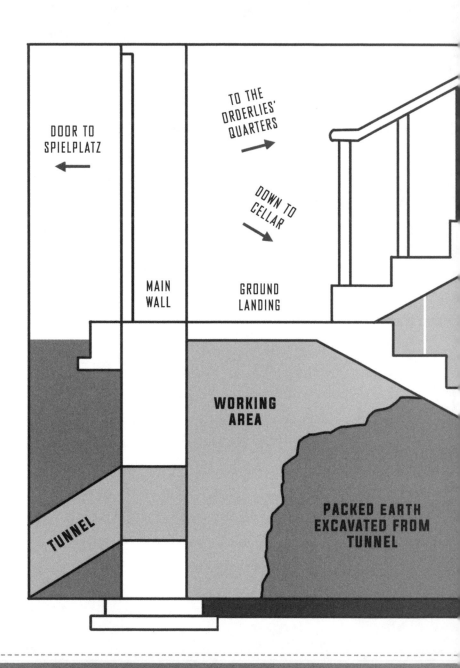

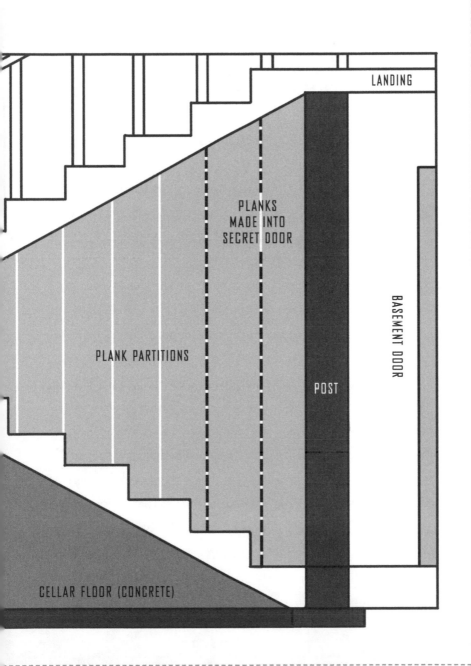

The ground, a compacted blend of yellow clay, dirt, and loose rock, was tough to burrow through, but they still managed to cut about a foot a day. By the time Gray returned to Holzminden, the tunnel was now approaching the eastern wall and the excavated debris nearly filled up the entire space underneath the stairs. They had made remarkable progress, and now it was his turn to do his bit, no matter his reluctance to enter the dark hole.

Gray knelt down by the tunnel entrance. First he pushed the shallow washbasin they used to collect the dirt from their digging into the hole. Then he followed it, lamp in hand. The earth closed around him like a tomb.

At Christmas, Colquhoun announced that the tunnel now ran beyond the wall and would soon be finished. They should all finish preparing their escape kits and be ready in the New Year.

There were great celebrations throughout camp for the holidays. The men sang carols, handed out homemade cards, raised money for the British Red Cross, staged a pantomime of *Sleeping Beauty*, and assembled a feast. Despite Niemeyer's ban on the sale of wine, Douglas Lyall Grant, of the London Scottish Regiment, supplied a cellar's worth of bottles that he joked cost more than a night out at London's swanky Carlton Hotel. At one point, such was their revelry—clapping hands, stomping feet, howls to the heavens—that they suspected their party must have been heard in town.

Holzminden theater performances.

The following morning, Boxing Day, Niemeyer announced that 20 officers, most of them prisoners since 1914, were being sent off by train to Holland. After half a year of promises, internment transfers had finally started. Some of the men slated to leave were part of the tunneling party. They shared farewells at the gate, and many other old-timers hoped they would be next.

But into this cascade of goodwill and good news came a terrible surprise in the form of a new security measure. Without explanation, Niemeyer ordered guards to take up permanent stations outside the stone walls. When the guards took their new positions, the tunnelers' hearts sank. One was standing opposite the east postern gate, on almost the exact location Colquhoun had planned for their tunnel exit. Had someone informed on their tunnel? Could they still manage to escape from that spot if they waited for a shift rotation? Would the guard stations be temporary? There had been no intensive search, so it was likely their secret was safe. They watched day after day to see if the guards abandoned their new posts; they remained.

The consequence was profound. To extend the tunnel beyond this new guard's line of sight, they would have to tunnel another 45 yards, under a barren flat field, until they reached some rows of rye—which would only provide cover come July, six months later. Otherwise—as the tunnelers knew well—they risked a bullet when they emerged from the ground. At a foot a day, this distance calculated to almost 20 more weeks of digging. Such a long time would make keeping the tunnel secret almost impossible. One errant word, one vigilant guard—and all would be lost.

Then there was the sap itself. A 15-yard tunnel was a manageable affair, but at 60 yards, cave-ins would be more likely, as would the chance of obstructions that demanded a change in direction. The time spent underground would become even more insufferable. The farther they dug, the longer it would take to wriggle in and out of the hole—and the more exhausting it would be. Such long periods in such cramped space so far from a safe retreat would be both physical and mental torture. A sap of that distance would run short of fresh air.

Some in the team lost heart, but not Gray, one of its senior leaders. He was determined to continue. They would need more men. Gray knew Caspar Kennard would be eager to join.

Caspar Kennard wriggled on his belly through the tunnel. Dragging a sack of tools and the circular basin behind him, he used his forearms and the toes of his boots to move himself through the tight, low burrow. Cascades of loosened dirt fell down into his collar. The dirt stung his eyes and gritted his mouth. None of this discomfort was much compared to the rising swell of fear that seized him. He hated confined spaces, and even though every instinct told him to break loose from this burrow, to retreat, he continued ahead.

On reaching the tunnel face, he lodged his tin-can lamp into the dirt by his side and drew out the gauge the tunnelers used to maintain a consistently sized hole. Too small, they would not be able to crawl through without causing a collapse. Too big, they would waste time excavating too much dirt that would have to be hauled out and stored away. The gauge was of basic construction: two thin boards—one 18 inches long, the other 14 inches—secured by a pivot at the center. Kennard swung the boards open until they formed a cross and placed them in front of him, the shorter board vertical and the longer horizontal. The ends marked the boundaries of their roughly oval tunnel. Once the gauge was fixed, he began to dig, using a chisel and trowel to scrape, stab, and pry loose the earth ahead of him. Progress was almost imperceptible, akin to emptying a bucket of water with a thimble. Only the slowly rising mound of dirt and stone under his chin gave any sign of progress.

When this mound impeded him, it was time for the basin at his feet. He stretched his arm under his body, rotating at the torso to lengthen his reach. As he moved, the roof and walls scattered dirt all over him. He dragged the basin up beside him. The exercise of such a simple task in such a small space was exhausting. Kennard's fear of the walls closing in on him only heightened the strain. After scooping the mound of soil into the basin with his hands, he screwed his body sideways again to push the basin back down to his feet. Then he tugged at its attached rope so his mates knew to haul it out. A moment later, the shallow basin skittered and danced its way into the darkness behind him.

He took a brief rest from the strain of maintaining a constant fixed position on his belly, arms out ahead of him, neck craned. He was sweating heavily, his nerves frayed. After he had advanced a little farther, he stopped digging and made a brace for the ceiling and walls. These braces were placed every three

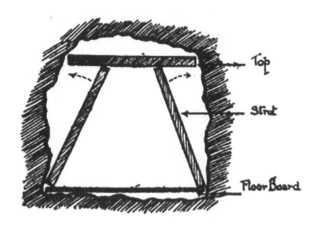

Top

Strut

Floor Board

1 ft. 6 in.

2 ft.

Illustrations of riveting a tunnel with wooden struts to keep it secure.

feet to prevent a collapse. He had brought some planks down with him, nicked from the support boards of barrack-room beds and cut to size. The tunnelers had taken so many that new arrivals to Holzminden often found their beds collapsing under them if they sat down too quickly. First, he wedged a board into the roof. On the floor he set another of the same length. The third he angled between the two horizontals, then knocked with his fist until it stood on the left side of the tunnel. He did the same on the right.

DOUBLE-DECKED BEDS

Illustration of a double-decked prisoner bed, ransacked for escape supplies.

Kennard's life had shifted in such strange and unimaginable ways over the past two years: from ranching in the open ranges of the Argentinean Pampas, to flying in the wide blue skies over England and France, to trading one solitary-detention cell for another. Not one of those cells could compare to the dreary darkness of this sap. But since recruitment to the secret effort early in the New Year, he had managed his claustrophobia. There was no better way out, no better way to get a head start before a manhunt was launched than a tunnel like this. His own impetuous run through the escape hatch had proved this fact.

CHAPTER 12

Most of the prisoners at Holzminden had no intention of burrowing a tunnel or concocting an elaborate breakout scheme. They filled their hours in other ways, taking advantage of the small liberties that Niemeyer allowed them. Some of them checked books out from the bustling library—its diligent attendant had collected almost 5,000 volumes. Others joined study circles to discuss architecture or the evolution of man. Some took classes taught by other prisoners practiced in farming, construction engineering, bookkeeping, horse management, and town planning as well as French, Russian, German, and even Portuguese.

There were hockey teams knocking about on a half-sized oblong ice pond formed on the Spielplatz, and officers threw one another around in jujitsu classes. Bridge and poker sessions ran around the clock, often fueled by too much wine, and there was even a knitting circle. Several prisoners became amateur painters and sketch artists. They also formed an orchestra. "There was a man there who seemed to be able to play anything," one orchestra member said. "He taught me the double-bass and trombone. The orchestra kept me going . . . It kept our spirits up; it would have been terrible if we'd just had to mooch about all day long."

The ice pond at Holzminden, for skating.

The orchestra accompanied the upstart "Gaiety Theatre," which Niemeyer finally permitted, perhaps in part because it gave his guards free entertainment. A rotating cast of prisoners turned actors from the "British Amateur Dramatic Society" put on variety shows and plays in the dining hall of Block B, pushing together the tables to make a stage. Besides actors, the theater occupied a small army of prisoners who became practiced stage hands, set designers, costume makers, and directors. James Whale, who would later become famous for his early Hollywood films *Frankenstein* and *The Invisible Man*, got his start in drama at Holzminden. "Pots of paint, wigs, flats, and all the properties in true Bohemian confusion," he wrote. "And yet on show nights they jumped together like magic."

There was a multitude of characters at Holzminden from all over the British Empire. One captive described "a motley crew": "Australians—South Africans—Canadians—New Zealanders— Irish—Scotch—English and Welsh." Every branch of the armed services was there too: pilots, cavalrymen, infantry, engineers, sappers, and garrison gunners. They came in all categories of personality. "The intellectuals regard with disdain the flighty scandalmongers. The foxtrot outfit squabbles with the church-goers, both requiring the same room at the same time for their widely different purposes. Then there are the drunks and the bluc ribald army—the studious and the do-noughts—the night birds and the gamesters."

"PARCELS!"

OR

"IF YOU DON'T WANT THE GOODS
DON'T MESS 'EM ABOUT!"

A MUSICAL COMEDY,
IN A BOX CONSISTING OF A LID AND
A BOTTOM CONTAINING FOUR TINS

BOOK AND LYRICS BY { D. G. GOLD.
G. R. EDWARDS.

PRODUCED BY G. R. EDWARDS.

UNDER THE MANAGEMENT OF THE B. A. D. S.

AT

THE GAIETY THEATRE

HOLZMINDEN.

NOTE: — THE PRODUCTION IS IN NO WAY INTENDED TO
REFLECT UPON THE EXCELLENT WORK DONE
BY THOSE WHO SEND US PARCELS FROM HOME.

A Gaiety Theatre program.

The arrival in December 1917 of Harold Medlicott bolstered the mood throughout the camp, for the breakout artists and those not interested alike. Medlicott was Britain's answer to Harry Houdini and had almost a dozen breakouts under his belt, several in broad daylight. One time he slid down the outside of a castle tower: His cell at its top was so high that the Germans did not believe it needed bars. Another time he rigged a plank of wood straight out from a second-floor window to cross a deep moat surrounding an old prison fortress. The officers believed that if anybody could escape Holzminden and shame Niemeyer, Medlicott was the man. A legend to even the German guards, he had broken out of nine camps already, never using the same method twice. With his usual bluster, Niemeyer assured Medlicott that Holzminden was escape-proof, a declaration that guaranteed his success would be all the sweeter for the whole camp.

On Sunday, February 10, Medlicott and his partner, Captain Joseph Walter, were all set to go, their plan timed to the second. At 3:30 p.m., wearing old Burberry jackets, rucksacks looped over their shoulders, they emerged from Block B. All was normal in the camp. Officers warmed their hands around the cookhouse stoves; some strolled about the Spielplatz. Patrolling guards paced the grounds. Nobody paid the two any mind. In the bright light of day, they made a hard right turn and crossed the gap between the two barrack blocks. Without hesitation, they lifted the single strand of wire that marked no-man's-land. At the barbwire fence, a few feet beyond, they bent down and quickly cut a hole. The orderly Dick Cash had provided the needed wire cutters—he traded food with a German workman for them.

Prisoners spotted the brazen move from the windows of both barrack blocks. At first they could not quite comprehend what they were seeing. Two sentries were walking a beat in the no-man's-land behind each barrack block—surely they would notice the two prisoners. Then they realized that the guards were walking away from each other, headed to the western and eastern ends of each barrack block, their backs to the two escapees. Once the guards reached the end of the blocks, however, they would turn around and come back. If they heard anything and turned early, Medlicott and Walter would be lost.

Still Medlicott and Walter continued. They were now at the northern wall. Medlicott hoisted his partner up on his shoulders, and Walter snipped a hole in the barbwire palisade. As soon as the hole was complete, he passed the wire cutters down to Medlicott, pushed through his rucksack, then crawled through the hole after it. Still, there was no whistle of alarm. Medlicott threw the wire cutters back across no-man's-land for Cash to retrieve. Then, just as the two guards made their reverse turn, he scaled the wall like a spider and dove through the hole in the palisade. The sentry beyond the walls must have been out of sight as well, since, again, there was no shout of alarm. Outside, they stood calmly by the wall, unfolded gentlemanly Homburg hats from inside their jackets, lit cigarettes, and started down the road like two villagers out for a Sunday afternoon stroll.

Medlicott and Walter would have made it away except that a sharp-eyed German guard watching over the isolation cells in Block B had, through a small, high window, seen them mount the wall. By the time he ran up the steps into the yard, the two breakout artists had turned off the road and were heading toward some woods half a mile away. They were still within sight of the camp when the alarm was raised. At first, they kept to a fast walk, hoping they might yet be mistaken for civilians. When guards poured out of the main gate and headed in their direction, they quickened into a jog. Soldiers from a nearby garrison, alerted by telephone by Niemeyer, cut them off before they reached the woods. Niemeyer met them in the yard, flushed with pride. He clapped his hand to the escapees' chests and declared, "All my boys come back to me."

When the officers standing in the windows would not be quiet, Niemeyer ordered his guards to fire at the barracks. Nobody was hit, but the crashing glass forced everyone to back away. Medlicott and Walter were brought down into the cellars and were not seen again at Holzminden before being sent away. At the next roll call, puffed with pride at the capture of the great Harold Medlicott, Niemeyer boasted about his "unblemished record" of there having been no successful home runs to Holland. But if he thought that the foiled attempt had crushed the morale of any who would dare to be next, he was wrong. As one prisoner wrote to Medlicott's family, the staggeringly brave display only proved to them all that "it was impossible for the Germans to confine a determined man."

In late February 1918, the tunnel plot ran into trouble yet again. The sap was some 25 yards long when the men began to run into roots and flat rocks embedded in hard clay. Progress slowed, and the men emerged after their shifts with cuts to their hands and covered with bruises from bumping their arms, legs, and heads against the stones. They believed they may have run into an ancient riverbed. At the same time, their team was falling apart.

Since the Boxing Day announcement about prisoners being transferred to internment in Holland, similar declarations came almost weekly. Often these were contradicted the very next day—names dropped, dates postponed. Moysey, Rogers, Ellis, Colquhoun, and a handful of the original tunnelers received word to pack their bags. Rather than welcoming the news, they were devastated. They had spent their time in captivity risking death, suffering solitary confinement, and exhausting themselves—all with an eye on escape. They saw the transfer as failure, especially since, under the terms of the agreement between the Germans and the Allies, released soldiers were forbidden to return to the battlefield. Further, although they would be free from Niemeyer and the trials of Holzminden, they would be leaving their friends behind in Germany. As Colquhoun said, "I felt like a deserter, nothing more or less." Given the choice, he would gladly have traded his place with someone else.

At the end of February, Gray said his good-byes to Colquhoun and the Pink Toes. They left the sap in his hands, and so he became the "Father of the Tunnel." Only Kennard and Frederick Mardock of the Royal Naval Air Service (RNAS) remained from the original team. Now, Gray needed not only to figure out how to burrow through the layers of rock, but also to assemble a whole new band of tunnelers while he was at it. Thanks to Hänisch sending the most diehard escape artists to Holzminden, he had a long list from which to choose.

In March, a new prisoner arrived with the boldness and experience they needed: Cecil Blain. He had spent over two months digging a tunnel at Neunkirchen, another prison camp. After it was discovered, he had vowed to never tunnel again. He quickly broke this vow to be with Kennard and Gray, working together again at long last. They were glad to have him.

Blain clawed the dirt to drag himself forward. Every so often, a rat scurried across his back or stared him straight in the eye. Worms and other unseen creepy-crawlies squirmed through his hair and underneath his work outfit, which stuck to him like a mildewed second skin. And the air . . . there was never enough to fill his lungs as he forged his way around the sandstone wall that had slowed and diverted the sap for weeks. As he advanced, he made sure to limit the swing of his elbows, the kick of his feet, the rise of his back. One indiscreet move in an unlucky spot, and the walls or roof might give in under the weight of the earth above. There would be no warning, no thunder boom to announce the cave-in. The dirt would simply cover him like a heavy shroud, immobilizing his body with its terrible weight, snuffing out his breath before he could cry for help.

At last, he arrived at the tunnel face. Slowly, but with a certain rhythm, he hacked with a chisel at the wall ahead, scraped away the loose chunks with a trowel, then filled the bowl with the excavated earth using a small hand rake. Part of him enjoyed it—the danger, the toil, the teamwork—it was an adventure and a better way to spend his days than sitting in the barracks . . . as long as the candle wedged into the wall by his side continued to flicker and dance. If the flame ever dulled into a faint red, he was in trouble.

Back by the tunnel entrance, Gray was keeping the candle— and Blain—alive. Crouched in a small cave carved into an early left turn in the sap, he operated what might best be described as a bellows. As the tunnel lengthened past the sandstone wall, the diggers found that they were growing faint from lack of oxygen. A few went delirious and had to be dragged out by their feet. Some method to supply fresh air was needed. Someone dreamed up a bellows made out of wooden planks and a leather RFC jacket, set on a vertical stand. To pipe the air to the tunnel face, they collected round shaving tins, knocked out the ends, strung them together, and covered them with canvas. Links were added as needed. Being the pumper was monotonous, arduous work.

Kennard stood just a few feet away, inside the chamber underneath the staircase, holding a rope in his hand and waiting to feel its tug. He was responsible for hauling back the bowl of dirt and stone when Blain was ready to send it back. He emptied its

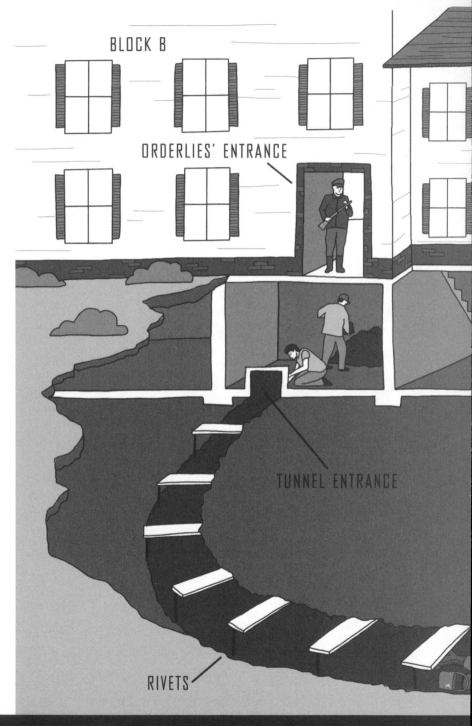

BLOCK B

ORDERLIES' ENTRANCE

TUNNEL ENTRANCE

RIVETS

Illustration showing a cross-section of the beginning of the tunnel—and its cramped quarters.

contents into cloth sacks and stacked them in the steadily shrinking space inside the chamber. On a good, well-run shift, the digger would have another pile to put in the bowl by the time the packer was ready to have him pull it back.

During their four-hour shift, Blain, Gray, and Kennard rotated through the jobs. Being the digger for too long was simply not sustainable, particularly for the claustrophobe Kennard, who had to bend every shred of his will to maintain his calm. The exertion, the foul air, the press of earth in every direction, the threat of collapse, all took their toll. To exit the tunnel, the digger had to snake backward, feet first, inch by inch through the tunnel to be free of it. There was simply no space to turn around.

At 3:45 p.m., the shift was over. The three men shed their grungy work outfits, wiped their skin clear of dirt with a cloth, and dressed in their orderly uniforms. Now they had to sneak back to their quarters. At this late afternoon hour, guards often used the stairs, bringing supplies up or down from the cellars. Through the thin breaks in the plank wall, the tunnelers could see them pass. Eventually, an orderly rapped on the secret door, then whispered, "Come out now."

The three men unlatched the slide bolt and stepped out through the plank door. At first the light stung their eyes. Then they hurried up the steps as the orderly returned the bolt into place. At the exit, they waited for one of their lookouts to give them another all-clear. With the single word "Right," the three moved out, forcing themselves to not so much as glance at the guard opposite the door. If he got a look at their faces, he might recognize one of them. They tried not to walk too fast or too slowly, relying on others from their team to intercept and distract any Germans who might cross their path. At last, they were back in Room 24, where they quickly changed back into their officer uniforms, famished, exhausted, and suffering stabbing headaches from the terrible air.

CHAPTER 13

Whether walking in the yard, sitting in their rooms, or working their shifts, the tunnelers continually hashed out how, once through the sap, they would make it across the 150 miles to the border. In fact, the distance they would have to travel as fugitives would be far greater given the detours needed to avoid towns and major roads. Gray was particularly aware that most escapes fell apart in this phase. Day and night, he considered different plans, searching for something foolproof.

Most of the tunnelers were banding up in teams for the flight to Holland, and Gray was committed to going with Blain and Kennard. He would not do a solitary run again; his own from Crefeld had proved to him how important it was to have partners who would look out for one another. There were few braver, tough, and more cool-headed when it mattered than Blain and Kennard. Travel by train Gray discounted, chiefly because a mass breakout would result in Niemeyer dispatching police to every nearby station and alerting conductors to confront any suspicious passengers. This left a journey by foot. Moving at night and hiding out during the day limited their chances of discovery, but Gray also knew that there was almost no way to cover such a distance without being spotted and forced into some kind of interaction. They would need disguises and cover stories.

People to avoid in escaping from Germany, by one who didn't
F. W. Voelcker,
Lieut. King's Shropshire Light Inf.

"Ludwig the Landsturmman". "Hans the Hound."

"Ferdinand the Forester." "Wilhelm the Wachtmeister." "Marie the Mädchen."

A helpful pamphlet on whom to avoid when escaping a German prison camp.

Gray spoke German fluently, but Blain and Kennard would have far more trouble. Blain had Cape Dutch from his time in South Africa and could make an attempt at answering some simple questions, but Kennard was unable to manage more than a few prepared phrases. Knowing this, Gray considered a plan where he would act as an officer escorting a pair of privates. Given his rank, he would be expected to answer for them. However, if challenged to any degree by a higher official, Blain and Kennard might be required to speak, and then they would be in trouble. Further, their uniforms would never remain sufficiently clean to pass for military inspection after they had tramped through woods and slept out of doors. No, Gray decided, they needed a plan that was sure to convince any doubters. Something extraordinary.

There was a lot to do in preparation. They needed good maps and compasses as well as food for 15 days of travel and Tommy cookers to heat their meals. They needed warm clothes and tough boots. They needed waterproof sacks to get their belongings across the river Weser. There were documents to forge, clothes to tailor, photographs to take. In the unoccupied Room 83, the tunnelers assembled a veritable escape factory—or, as they called it, "a temple to the Goddess of Flight." They hid items under floorboards and behind sliding paneled walls, along with all manner of equipment used in their preparations, including locksmithing and woodworking tools, a sewing machine, and dyes, inks, and paper for passes. They had built their tunnel bellows in this room. By mid-April they were hard at work making passes and creating backpacks from old jackets smeared with lard.

In all these efforts, they had help. Since first arriving at Holzminden, officers had bribed and inveigled some of the guards and other staff, turning them into willing accomplices who provided information or special items. Niemeyer's poor treatment of his men made them easy turncoats. As one British officer described, when the commandant tired of abusing his prisoners, he vented his "black gusts of bilious passion" on his staff, often leaving them "literally trembling as he flayed

Moccasins made by Holzminden POW Edward Leggatt for his escape.

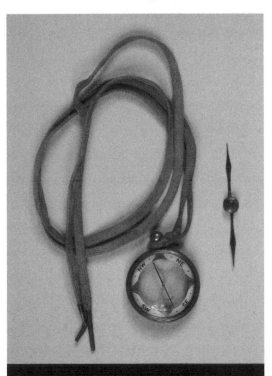

A compass used by Leggatt during his escape attempt.

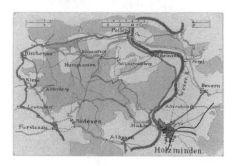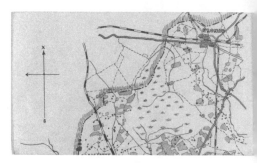

Leggatt's escape maps.

them with his tongue." The war's harsh economic rationing was added motivation.

"Letter Boy," the commandant's clerk, was easily charmed with coffee and cookies. His work delivering letters gave him free rein to move about the barracks, and he met almost daily with the conspirators to pass along the latest intelligence or material he purchased on their behalf. What was more, he always knew when searches were coming and where they would occur. The "Sanitary Man" was the only civilian at Holzminden who could go about without a guard accompanying him. In exchange for some cash and something from Fortnum & Mason—the upmarket London grocery store—he would shop in town for any goods the prisoners requested. "The Typist," a young secretary in the Kommandantur, helped them for less mercenary reasons. She had fallen in love with Peter Lyon, a 6-foot-3 Australian infantry officer who was a member of the tunnel conspiracy.

Since his capture in spring 1917, Lyon had lost over 60 pounds because of an insufficient diet, but none of his good looks. Between exchanging love notes, the Typist provided sample passes and the paper stock on which they were printed. Finally, there was Kurt Grau, a well-meaning camp interpreter. He had been stationed in India and once proclaimed, "I do not care for Germany. I do not care for England. My heart is in India." As Gray had served a number of years in the army there, not to mention it being his birthplace, he was able to convince Grau that he could help set him up in India when the war was over. Grau became a friend to their cause.

The tunnelers benefited as well from their continued alliance with several orderlies. Beyond providing access to their quarters, these men also helped with the escape factory. With his photography experience, Dick Cash was foremost among them. Not only did the officers need photographs for their passes, they each needed a copy of a map for their journey. It was one thing to chart a general westward course and quite another to have a map to identify every village, road, waterway, and town they came across. The ability to do so might separate success from recapture. They had managed to smuggle into Holzminden a large military map that covered the expanse of territory they would cross. Cash made a shopping list: camera, plates, chemicals, printer paper, and a carbide bike lamp to develop the film. He started collecting what he needed. Each week, Gray asked for additional copies of the map, because as the sap lengthened the number of officers brought into the fold increased.

Protocol required that Lieutenant Colonel Rathborne, as senior British officer after Wyndham had been sent to another camp, be informed of the plan. What was more, he could use his position to stall other attempts that might result in their tunnel's discovery. Gray also knew that Rathborne was keen to escape himself. When notified, Rathborne not only gave his blessing but volunteered to join the scheme and to help in any way he could. Others were brought in to stand lookout as well as to obtain boards to brace the tunnel walls, sacks to pack dirt into, and tins to extend the ventilation pipe. With each additional member, the chance of exposure grew, but Gray accepted the risk. There was no other way to build a tunnel of that length and to orchestrate a well-prepared, properly supplied home run to Holland.

One afternoon, Gray finally struck upon an idea for his own escape run with Blain and Kennard. He was in the tunnel chamber with the two of them, and they were getting ready to start their shift. Kennard lit a candle and knelt down by the sap entrance. Looking into the dark hole, he muttered, "We must be bloody mad."

"That's it!" Gray exclaimed. Blain and Kennard looked at their usually taciturn friend as if he had suddenly lost the run of himself. "Mad!" Gray chuckled. "Mad! That's the answer. It simply couldn't miss!" The other two tried to get him to explain, but he told them that he wanted to think on it some more, to investigate its faults and merits. "Come on, let's get on with it," he said, taking the candle from Kennard. "I think I've come up with the answer to our prayers, that's all." With that, he crawled into the tunnel, the first digger of the day.

Then a run of bad luck and imprudence put everything in jeopardy.

First, rumors of the scheme began to filter throughout the camp. With roughly two dozen individuals in the know as well as the strange movements of officers in and out of their quarters, keeping their activities secret was impossible. But it was one thing to hear a rumor and quite another to know exactly where the tunnel was located. An orderly known to spy for Niemeyer in exchange for gifts of wine began asking around camp about where the tunnel's entrance was hidden. It was too great a risk for the tunnelers, and one night, while drunk, the orderly "accidentally" tumbled down the steps in Block B and cracked his skull. He never made another inquiry.

In mid-May, Niemeyer instituted reprisals in response to restrictions put in place against German officers in Britain. Worst of these, for the tunnelers, was a new schedule of roll calls. Instead of twice a day at 9 a.m. and 4 p.m., the prisoners were now forced to gather on the Spielplatz at 9 a.m., 11:30 a.m., 3:30 p.m., and 6 p.m. These frequent roll calls cut straight into the middle of the four-hour tunnel shifts. At first the tunnelers tried standing in for those on shift. When the names of the working crew were called, their mates answered for them, then moved down the line to respond to their own names. They pulled it off for a few days but were sure that continuing the charade day after day would see them caught.

They began to rush to and from their digging sessions between the 11:30 and 3:30 roll calls, the time of the day when most guards were away from Block B for lunch. Roll calls took at least a half hour, which meant that, even hurrying, the teams of three had less than two hours underground. Their recklessness quickly cost them. One day, after finishing a shift, a working party was hurrying out of the east door of Block B without taking the usual precautions, and one of the officers was recognized by a passing guard. The guard tried to stop the officer, but he rushed away into the barracks through his own entrance.

Niemeyer was informed of the incident, and a search of Block B followed, but the guard could not identify the officer in question. All the prisoners were ordered onto the Spielplatz, and an exhaustive inspection of the orderlies' barracks began. The tunnelers waited for the fateful moment when their secret door would be found. After a long time, the prisoners were ordered back into their barracks. Yet again, the door had eluded discovery. The tunnelers breathed easy at last. Upset that nothing had been found, Niemeyer vented his spleen on the guard who had failed to identify the officer, sending him to the jug for eight days. He also posted a permanent guard on the steps outside the orderlies' door. With this, the tunnelers lost their access point. It was a cruel blow.

They immediately decided to stop all activity. The Germans were on alert, and anything out of the ordinary was sure to raise suspicion. During that time, horrible news reached them via the Poldhu—Harold Medlicott and Joseph Walter had been murdered.

Having escaped from Bad Colberg camp in Saxony, some 150 miles south of Holzminden, they had been caught on the run. The camp commandant, a man called Kröner, had sent eight of his most fearsome men to get them at the local train station. Before leaving, one of them was overheard saying, "Yes, they are two very brave men, but they will be shot." Later that afternoon, the guards returned to the camp with two stretchers covered in dark sheets—clearly the dead bodies of Medlicott and Walter. According to Kröner, they had been shot in the Pfaffenholz forest after a "sudden dash for freedom" from the station.

The senior British officer at Bad Colberg demanded to see the bodies. If they had been killed in the manner reported, the nature of their wounds would match the story. Kröner refused. Then, while several British officers distracted the guards watching over the bodies, another officer rushed up and threw aside the sheets. Medlicott's and Walter's bodies were riddled with over a dozen bullets and stabbed with several bayonet wounds. It was evident that they had been murdered; Kröner's story was a patent lie.

The tunnelers in Holzminden had little doubt that they risked the same fate if they too were caught escaping. Niemeyer had proven himself time and again to use force—either by bayonet or bullet—to make a statement. But the prisoners were undaunted. They surveyed the barracks and grounds again, looking for another way down to their sap. Nobody lived in the attic of the officer section in Block B, and, as a result, the Germans were unlikely to inspect any of the rooms too closely. The double swing doors onto the floor were secured with a metal chain looped between the steel handles and a heavy padlock. Picking the padlock would be too time-consuming, but the handles themselves were only fastened to the door by six screws. Remove the screws, take off one handle, and they could access the floor. Afterward, replace the screws and handle, and nobody would be any the wiser.

There was a barricade separating their quarters from those of the orderlies, but they found a way to bypass it: the eaves. These ran the length of the barracks like a corridor under the steeply sloped roof. If they cut a panel in the wall in one of the rooms, they could use the eaves to reach the eastern side. This they quickly did, making the opening look seamless with the wall by using some mortar and distemper paint and hiding it behind an unused bed. Then they discovered a small door at the other end of the eaves that opened into an attic room where some of the orderlies slept. No doubt the original builders put it there to access the space. Not only did this solution return access to their tunnel in the cellars, it was a far superior approach. They would no longer need to risk masquerading as orderlies to get past the guards. More important, apart from showing up for roll calls, they could dig day and night.

And so they resumed work, quickly making up for lost time.

CHAPTER 14

A lunatic who had escaped from an insane asylum. This was the role Gray wanted Kennard to play on their journey to the border. He could rant and blubber, tear his hair out, convulse on the ground, talk in tongues or stay mute and wild-eyed, whatever he pleased—never would he need to speak intelligible German, nor would he be expected to answer questions. Gray and Blain would be the attendants escorting him back to the asylum.

At last Gray had revealed his plan, and from his answers to Blain's and Kennard's questions, it was clear he had thought it all through.

What insane asylum? There was an institution in the town of Vechta, roughly 45 miles east of the Dutch border. It was north of the most direct route to the Netherlands, but the extra miles were worthy of the ruse. *What if they were stopped by the police or other officials?* Gray would act as the senior attendant, making any explanations in German. If they were pushed too far, or if Blain was asked to speak, Kennard would provide the perfect distraction. He could stage an episode, wrestling against his restraints, shaking and foaming at the mouth. His attendants would need to control him, perhaps even force a "tranquilizer" (aspirin, but who would be any the wiser?) into his mouth. Locals would want to be rid of them quickly. *How would they explain traveling by foot and not by train?* Kennard was too dangerous to be trusted around civilians. This would also explain the rumpled, dirty state of their clothes. After all, the lunatic had been on the run, Gray and Blain had tracked him down, and ever since they had been returning on foot. *What would they wear exactly?* According to what Gray had learned from his inquiries, patients at Vechta wore simple gray shirts and pants with peaked caps. As attendants, he and Blain would wear plain civilian suits. All were easily crafted at Holzminden.

Try as they might, Blain and Kennard could not poke any holes in the plan. Of all the disguises they had known their fellow escape artists to use, it was by far the most original. Gray would be Franz Vogel, senior attendant at Vechta Asylum. Blain: Karl Holzmann, junior attendant. Kennard: Kurt Grau, the lunatic. Kennard took the name of the German interpreter who had assisted Gray in gathering all the information he needed to pull off the ruse. Satisfied with the plan, the three started to prepare the clothes and passes they would need. As an escapee, Kennard would not need papers, but Gray and Blain made identity cards with the names of their aliases, the papers stamped and signed with the name of Vechta's chief of police, Günther. They had an official letter, also signed by "Günther," explaining the nature of their business: "We hereby certify that the two guards Karl Holzmann and Franz Vogel (Chief Guard) have the job of transporting the lunatic Kurt Grau to the asylum at Vechta. The above lunatic is forbidden to travel by rail or other public transport and may not meet other people. All policemen and officials

Blain's escape map, fake ID, and fake papers.

are earnestly requested to give all possible help in transporting this lunatic to his destination."

The others in the breakout team banded up in twos and threes and gathered what they could in supplies. One officer's escape kit, stored in a host of hiding places about the barracks, was typical: one compass, one map, one Tommy cooker, one Dixie cup, nine hard-boiled eggs, five pounds of chocolate, eight sausages in skins, two tins of Oxo cubes, one tin of chocolate powder, one tin of tea tablets, one tin of saccharin, one and a half pounds of dried fruit, 16 ration biscuits, shaving tackle, soap, mending material, two pairs of spare socks, one bottle of water, one piece of biltong (dried meat), one steel saw. Others also had cigarettes, flashlights, German marks, rope, brandy cherries, oats, silk underwear, and other comforts for what threatened to be a long, hard trail. The men tested their homemade waterproof rucksacks by floating them in a large tin bath. "Bone dry," one tunneler declared after the test.

Rathborne intended to go by train, a respectable businessman on a cross-country journey. He had little to prepare: two civilian suits and a leather satchel that held some food, a razor, soap, a towel, a hairbrush, and a hand mirror. To top off his look, he purchased a felt hat accented by a feather (in "true German style," he explained) and borrowed some spectacles from a roommate. Cash completed his stack of maps, and the tunnelers pored over every line and marker, scouting the route they would take to the border to avoid the manhunt that was sure to follow.

Escape equipment sent to Holzminden, including compasses, wire cutters, maps showing potential routes to the Dutch border, and lead to conceal the weight, hidden in a tin of ox tongue.

The tunnelers were not alone in their hopes and dreams, though—summer escape fever hit Holzminden just as the weather turned warm. On June 6, three prisoners hid inside a rubbish cart that was due to be collected and brought out of the camp. They were caught before it reached the gate. Days later, two diehard breakout fiends, Timothy Brean and Cuthbert Sutcliffe, made their own attempt—in more glamorous fashion. Sutcliffe, whose nickname was "Fluffy," often took the female roles in the camp's plays. He had grown his hair past his shoulders, ostensibly to better play the parts, but he had ulterior

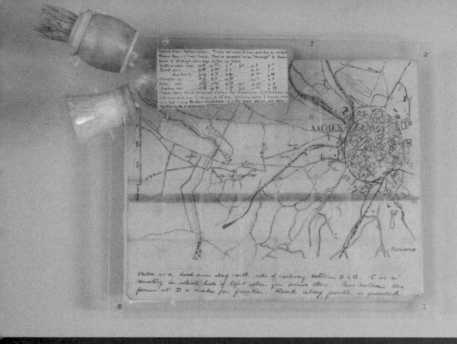

Holzminden escape equipment, including a railway timetable and map of the surrounding area, hidden in a shaving brush.

reasons. Hair curled, cheeks rouged, and dressed up like a "girl typist," Sutcliffe broke through the barricade in Block A into the Kommandantur. Brean followed, dressed in a pristine German officer's uniform. As they headed out the barrack entrance, Brean acted like he was dictating notes to his typist, and Sutcliffe sashayed out the gate, attracting nothing more than the admiring gazes of the guards. However, Brean was recognized as a British officer, and the two were snatched up.

None of these prisoners had informed Rathborne, the senior officer, about their plans, and their attempts caused fear to stab at the tunnelers that another search or punishment order would stall—or, worse, uncover—their own efforts, particularly since rumors about a sap still persisted. Anticipating a search, they kept constant watch for any movements around the camp that were out of the ordinary.

Compounding this anxiety, Niemeyer had the whole camp riled up over his treatment of Captain William Leefe Robinson— an RFC pilot who had destroyed a German Zeppelin on a bombing raid over England, killing its 16 German crew members but undoubtedly saving many British lives. Since Robinson came to Holzminden in mid-May 1918, Niemeyer had made it his mission

'THREE MORE OUT.'

A creative escape attempt.

to break him. He had rarely seen the outside of a solitary cell, and when he did, Niemeyer forced him daily from his bed at bayonet point, inflicted additional roll calls on him, restricted his movements, demeaned him in front of camp visitors, and whipped him in private. Niemeyer's treatment of Robinson had every British officer spoiling for a fight.

With these incidents and the burden of leading the tunnel project at its most critical hour, Gray was uncharacteristically on edge when one day he found himself confronted by an irksome German attendant in the parcel room. Something about his tone, or look, or the way he mishandled packages set Gray off. The two exchanged words, and the attendant grabbed the British pilot. The level-headed reaction would have been to submit, particularly at such a crucial time as this, but Gray had had enough. He rooted himself to the floor and refused to budge. Shouts of alarm brought a host of German guards. Perhaps to shield his embarrassment at being unable to manage the situation, the attendant accused Gray of brandishing a large knife that had remained on the table throughout the short scuffle. Gray was hauled down to a solitary cell, and Niemeyer sent him to Hanover for a court-martial.

For once, the scales of justice tipped in favor of a British prisoner, and Gray received only two weeks' solitary imprisonment for "simple disobedience." Through Captain Hugh Durnford, a fellow Anglo-Indian officer who spoke Hindi and occupied a room in Block B right above his cell window, Gray was kept apprised on the tunnel's progress and relayed messages to the team. He urged Blain and Kennard to launch the escape once the sap reached the rows of rye, even if he was not yet free himself. They could not risk a delay. On one of the walls in Gray's cell was scribbled with the line, "Stone walls do not a prison make. Nor iron bars a cage." As he languished in the cellar, looking at those words, the tunnel approached its most critical hour.

CHAPTER 15

Jim Bennett, an RNAS observer, and his two shift mates crept from their rooms in Block B and climbed the stairs to the attic floor. Another officer accompanied them to unscrew the door-handle plate, let them through, then refasten the plate so the padlock and chain looked secure if a guard came by. The three men removed the panel in the unused attic room that gave access to the eaves, hurried down the sloped space, and exited on the orderlies' side. At the bottom of the stairs, they slipped through the narrow hidden door in the panel.

A half hour later, Bennett reached the face of the sap. The 26-year-old from Somerset, England, came from a family of farmers. He had been hunting for U-boats in the North Sea when his plane had mechanical trouble and crash-landed on the roiling waters. Bennett and his pilot were captured by the crew of a German submarine. In the almost year since, he had attempted to escape several camps before being sent to Holzminden. There, he was reunited with his pilot Peter Campbell-Martin, who was already in on the tunnel scheme. Bennett proved a tireless worker.

Now their new method of entry provided round-the-clock access, and the tunnelers really did need every minute. The "last lap" of their dig had proved to be the most difficult. This was not

Jim Bennett.

only because of the distance from the entrance to the end of the tunnel, but also because they had hit another layer of stones as they began to gradually angle the tunnel up toward the surface. After a long stint prying these stones loose from the hard clay, Bennett shimmied his way backward down to the start of the tunnel, to change places with one of his shift mates.

Several hours later, the three heaved their sacks over their shoulders and climbed back up the stairs. With the tunnel chamber packed from floor to ceiling with sacks of dirt and stone, they now had to carry out their excavated debris. They scattered the contents of the sacks about the eaves, then returned to their rooms. The finish seemed close enough to taste.

On June 30, the team figured that their tunnel extended into the rye field at last. By a length of parcel string, it measured almost 60 yards. Infantry lieutenant Walter "Basil" Butler volunteered to pinpoint the tunnel's exact position. He scrabbled through the hole while some others from the team watched from a fourth-floor window in Block B. For most of its distance, the tunnel ran nine feet underground, but the incline at the end brought it to within five feet of the surface. Butler had with him a long, rigid wire with a white cloth tied to its end. When he reached the face of the tunnel, he would push the wire's point up through the earth. The team scanned the field for any flash of the cloth. If the guard outside the wall spotted a dirty white flag suddenly emerging from the ground, they—and the tunnel— would be done for. After what seemed a lifetime, the cloth finally emerged. As Bennett described it, it "nosed its way up through the earth like some strange new plant." Then it quickly disappeared underground again. The sight, a full eight yards short of the field of rye and completely exposed in the wide open field, left the whole team crushed.

They had no choice than to keep digging. The rye field was farther than they had predicted, and all the rises and falls, twists and turns of their tunnel had thrown off their measurements as well. Any day, the tall stalks of rye might be harvested and their cover lost. Desperate, they worked shift after shift, with a frenzy that left them exhausted and rattled. Not only did they have to excavate another 24 feet of earth, but they also had to cut an offshoot chamber to house the dirt that would be brought down on the night they dug to the surface. One July day followed the next, the layer of compacted stones continuing to dog their

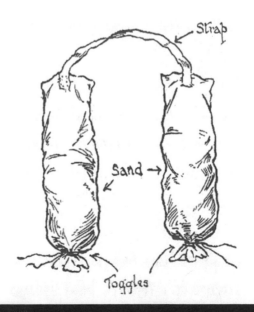

Illustration of a device for carrying sand and soil out underneath a coat.

efforts, and they had only advanced a few yards. They were simply not making the progress they needed.

Gray's two weeks of suffering the heat and small confines of solitary complete, he emerged from the cellar more resolved than ever to escape, and they held a late-night meeting in the barracks to bring him fully up to date. They still had six yards to go to reach the rye field, and the jeopardy to their plan of the approaching harvest was too great. The end of the sap was almost within reach of six rows of green beans that had been planted in front of the rye. Although they were only two feet high and were in range of the camp's arc lights, their dense bushy leaves would go some way to concealing the emergence of the escapees from the tunnel. If they crawled low enough—and, by now, all the officers were experts in that—they could get to the tall rye and away. After some debate, the men voted to revise their exit point. It was their only option.

In mid-July, as the sappers approached the bean rows, Niemeyer unwittingly helped them with their preparations by lifting the ban on parole walks. It was an odd sensation walking easily out of Holzminden when they had been laboring so hard underground. On one walk, their guard even allowed them to wade into the river Weser to cool off from the hot summer sun. Some of the tunnelers pushed deep into the water to find the easiest crossing point. The other restrictions were also lifted, and, after a month of not being allowed any theater, the prisoners were permitted to stage a revue, *Home John*, in the Block B dining hall. Some of the actors wore tuxes and evening dresses, and one, playing a statue of William Shakespeare, was in white robes and stood on top of a box engraved with the great dramatist's name. Even David Gray played a small role. It was almost as if he had no plans to escape in a few days' time.

Officers crowded into every available space to watch, and Niemeyer sent interpreters to make sure that no criticisms were made of the German Reich. During the intermission, a newly arrived prisoner turned to the fellow next to him and asked indiscreetly, within earshot of the interpreters, "Are you in on the tunnel?" The very utterance of the word sent a shockwave through the surrounding men, some of whom were indeed in on the scheme. The interpreters gave no sign of having heard, nor did anyone dare respond, but it was proof that the existence of the tunnel was common knowledge. There were whispers about

602

Ich gebe mein Ehrenwort, für den Fall meiner Beteiligung an einem Spaziergange, während des Spazierganges, d. h. vom Verlassen des Lagers bis zur Rückkehr in dasselbe nicht zu entfliehen, während der gleichen Zeit jeder Anordnung des Begleitpersonals nachzukommen und keine Handlungen zu begehen, die gegen die Sicherheit des Deutschen Reiches gerichtet sind. Ich weiss, dass nach § 159 des M.-St.-G.-B. ein Kriegsgefangener, der trotz abgegebenen Ehrenwortes entflieht, der Todesstrafe verfallen ist.

ich gebe auch mein Ehrenwort, diese Karte nur für mich zu gebrauchen und sie keinem anderen Gefangenen zu geben.

Holzminden, den *16. 2. 18.*

I, herewith, give my word of honour that I shall not, in case of my taking part in a walk, make an attempt of escape during such walk, i. e. from the time of leaving the camp until having returned to it, at the same time strictly obeying any orders given to me by the accompanying officer an not to commit any acts that are directed against the safety of the German Empire. I know, that according to § 159 of the M.-St.-G.-B. a prisoner of war, who escapes in despite of the word of honour given, is liable to death.

I give also my word of honour to use this card only myself and not to give it to any other prisoner of war.

Name: *L. J. Bennett*

Jim Bennett's Holzminden parole walk card.

Theater performance right before the escape at Holzminden.

it all through the camp. Prisoners who were unaware of the nature of the plan knew there was an escape in the offing. One recent arrival, who was pushing to be a part of whatever the plan might be, wrote in his diary, "Expecting something big to come off any night now ... The whole camp is getting kind of anxious."

Some rival schemes aimed to get out ahead of the tunnel crew, knowing that it would result in a crackdown. Rathborne made it his mission to deter these attempts. Soon after the revue, he got wind of a scheme in Block A. Several officers intended to short-circuit the camp lights at night. In the confusion that followed, a decoy would be hung from the windows on one side of the barracks, to look as if someone was climbing down to the yard, while the escapees cut the wire fences on the opposite side and dashed away. It was a clever idea, but Rathborne instructed its ringleader (call him "Livewire") to put a stop to it. Livewire resisted. Rathborne made it clear that the tunnel had been in the works for almost nine months, and that, as senior British officer, he was forbidding all other attempts until it had gone ahead. Livewire reluctantly agreed but asked to be part of the breakout. "Impossible," Rathborne said. Over the past several months, any tunnelers occupying rooms in Block A had gradually won transfers to Block B. At this late stage, any requests to be moved might raise suspicions in the Kommandantur. Rathborne won the argument again—or so he thought.

On July 21, the tunnelers scraped away their last horizontal length of dirt and stone. By their measurements, their sap reached beyond the first two rows of beans. The rectangular offshoot chamber that would store their upward diggings was also complete. At a meeting in the barracks that afternoon, the tunnelers decided that "Zero Hour" would be the following night, after lockup.

Gray led the meeting. He wanted an orderly breakout. Nothing could be left to chance. Any unnecessary bustle in the corridors of Block B, whether on the officer side or on that of the orderlies, might be noticed by a guard. He wanted no logjams in the eaves, the stairwell chamber, or, worst of all, the tunnel itself. The men would be on edge already, and he did not want a stampede or a scuffle to erupt, nor any panic within the sap. Every man must know his place in the line and when he was to move. There was to be a buffer of time to allow for any delays or hiccups along the way.

The first escape party would be the 13 officers who made up the team assembled after the departure of Colquhoun and the Pink Toes (with Blain as a late arrival). Once this baker's dozen was clear, the rest of the team would start to move. First off would be Rathborne. Then Bennett and Campbell-Martin, followed by John Bousfield and Lyon, and finally John Tullis, Stanley Purves, and Leggatt.

There were also others to consider: "the ruck." The team drew up a list of other officers who had contributed in some way to the escape. The more important their contribution, the higher on the list their name appeared. Outside of these individuals, each tunneler was allowed to nominate an officer they trusted to be included in the attempt. In total, there were sixty men on the list, almost 10 percent of the total camp population. To maintain secrecy, the men in the ruck would only be informed that the escape was in progress after lockup. Those willing to attempt an escape would be instructed to ready what kits they could and await the signal to go. Allowing the tunnelers a head start, the ruck would begin to move an hour after the last of the core team was out of the sap.

The orderlies were asked if they wanted to use the tunnel to escape themselves, but they were not willing to trade Holzminden for a coal or salt mine, which would surely be their punishment

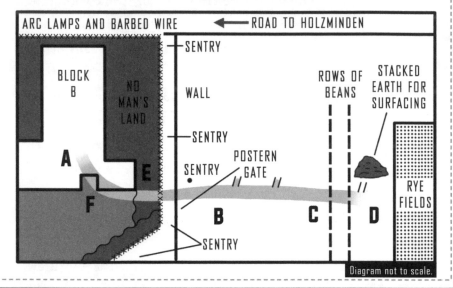

PROGRESSION OF THE TUNNEL

A=ENTRANCE TO TUNNEL **B**=FIRST PLANNED EXIT **C**=TEST EXIT BY BUTLER **D**=FINAL EXIT
E=WINDOW FROM WHICH TEST EXIT WAS OBSERVED **F**=ORDERLIES' ENTRANCE

ARC LAMPS AND BARBED WIRE ← ROAD TO HOLZMINDEN

BLOCK B

NO MAN'S LAND

A

E

F

SENTRY

WALL

SENTRY

SENTRY

POSTERN GATE

SENTRY

B

ROWS OF BEANS

STACKED EARTH FOR SURFACING

C

D

RYE FIELDS

Diagram not to scale.

if they were caught. It would be reward enough to know they had helped the tunnelers escape and had made Niemeyer look a fool. Two officers volunteered to oversee the escape operation. Captain Durnford, Rathborne's adjutant and a friend of David Gray, was selected to manage the list. He would be responsible for alerting each officer when it was time to go. Lieutenant Louis "Swaggy" Grieve would serve as doorman on the attic floor. Nobody would get past the short, barrel-chested Australian without his permission—not least because he was well loved by the whole camp for his Sydney cheer. On the other side of the eaves, four orderlies would take control: one to oversee flow out of the eaves, one to lead each officer down the stairwell, and two in the chamber itself, sending men into the tunnel. Their plan in place, the men concluded their meeting and went out to the Spielplatz for what they hoped would be one of their last roll calls in Holzminden.

The next night, the tunnelers ate the heartiest meals they could assemble, got dressed for their journey, and inspected their rucksacks one last time before cinching them closed. All had their journeys to the border planned. They waited for the guard who always made one last check of the corridors and rooms at night to finish and leave the barracks. Suddenly, Livewire, the ringleader of the Block A escape plot, was discovered hiding in Block B. He had heard that the breakout was scheduled to come off and planned to be a part of it. This could not be allowed to happen. First, Livewire was not on the list. Second, if it was discovered that he was missing from his own barracks during the final check of the night, an alarm would be raised.

Rathborne took control of the situation, ordering Livewire to go directly to the guard on duty and tell him that he had mistakenly stayed in Block B after lockup. He could say that he had lost track of time, that he had fallen asleep—whatever he decided— but he had to go. Defeated, Livewire left to take his medicine. To be on the safe side, the tunnelers postponed "Zero Hour" for the following night.

CHAPTER 16

"Tonight!" All through Tuesday, July 23, the tunnelers whispered this to one another. Roused from their beds and herded onto the Spielplatz for morning roll call. *"Tonight!"* Drinking tea, eating stale biscuits for breakfast, waiting in line for one last parcel or letter. *"Tonight!"* Shuffling about the yard, watching a game of football, a tasteless lunch. *"Tonight!"* Reading in their rooms, checking their kits again, playing poker, another roll call. *"Tonight!"* Another circle of the yard, a stretch of the legs, a pot of coffee. *"Tonight!"* The evening roll call, a final harangue from Niemeyer, murky brown soup for dinner. *"Yes: Tonight."*

At 6 p.m., Gray assembled the team in the barracks. Their long captivity was almost over, and they were anxious, knowing well the perils that lay ahead. They would go tonight, he confirmed. Everybody was to be ready after lockup. The halls and rooms were to be swept of any officers who did not belong in Block B. Lookouts would be posted at the entrance to ensure that neither Livewire nor any other interlopers tried to come inside. There could not be another postponement.

The tunnelers left to prepare, and Gray sat down with Durnford. The two men were of similar age and experience and shared a particular style: well-trimmed mustaches and a stiff look. A decorated officer of the Royal Field Artillery, Durnford had been captured in the Ypres Salient after getting lost amid the ruined, featureless landscape in August 1917. He had known about the tunnel for months but thought it nothing but a fool's errand, sure to be discovered. Now that it was finished, he regretted not being on the list, but he swore to do everything he could to see it come off smoothly.

The sky darkened, and clouds swept quickly across the rising moon—a storm was blowing in. Gray waited with Blain and Kennard in his room, where they passed the time until lockup, examining their maps again, making sure they knew exactly where they would go in the first few hours of their run to Holland. Blain turned his silver cigarette lighter over and over in his hand. He had prematurely inscribed it with the words, "Holzminden—Escaped July 22"—the previous night's date. Kennard practiced his madman act. He wandered about the room, rolling his eyes, jabbering incoherently, blowing spit bubbles, and whimpering like a wounded animal. "Oh, shut up and listen for a minute!" Gray interrupted at one point, drawing his attention back to the maps. Not even the Father of the Tunnel was immune to the tension of the night.

Throughout Block B, officers were nervously waiting. They ate what food they could stomach and smoked cigarettes. Some drank wine to bolster their courage. Others declined, believing alcohol would dull their senses and their reflexes when they needed them the most. Jim Bennett was one of those who stayed sober. In his mind, he played out the journey through the tunnel, then the swim across the Weser. Once on the opposite bank, he hoped to navigate quickly—and quietly—through the surrounding fields of corn and rye, eluding any pursuers.

Rathborne strode the barrack hallways, checking with the lookout at the door that there had been no more surprise visits from Livewire. He confirmed that there were no interlopers inside the barracks. Rathborne then dropped by Durnford's room to say good-bye. When he put on his feathered cap and glasses to show off his disguise, Durnford praised his look as "wonderfully Teutonic." Then he wished him good luck.

Blain and Kennard returned to their own bunks shortly before 9 p.m. They put on their escape outfits with their pajamas over them. The pajamas would keep their clothes clean while they were crawling through the tunnel. At the turn of the hour, the door to Block B was shut and locked on the inside by the lone guard. No matter how long the officers had been prisoners, that resonating clang never lost its impact. One hour more to wait. They kept an ear out for the footsteps of the guard. If they heard him coming into any of their rooms, the tunnelers knew to jump into bed and throw their blankets up over their clothes.

The minutes ticked away. The wind continued to gust, and the occasional flash of lightning lit up the sky. Rain had yet to fall, but it would start before long. If they did manage to break out, they would be soaked to the skin before they even reached the river. At 10 p.m., as was his routine, the guard finished his last check and exited the building, locking the door behind him. Fifteen minutes later, Gray informed Durnford that all was clear. Time to go. Durnford made his way through the corridors, alerting those in the ruck that the escape was going ahead and that each man should be ready when his time came. Some tried to cajole and bribe him to know their place on the list, but Durnford was incorruptible.

Boots in hand, all the better to keep quiet, and kit bags looped over their shoulders, the core group of tunnelers crept out of their rooms. Together, they climbed the stairs to the attic. The handle of the swing doors was removed, and they entered the attic floor. They assembled one last time in the room with the hidden panel. There was no need for speeches, nor any final instructions. They were all prepared for what lay ahead.

They wished each other well—Good luck, Godspeed—then Butler, the first on the list, disappeared into the eaves. Outside, the storm howled. As one officer described it, thunder cracked and boomed like the "finale of a gigantic orchestra." They could not have asked for better weather to sneak into the night.

A religious man, Butler muttered a short prayer before pushing his kitbag into the tunnel and following it in. He had crawled his way through the sap scores of times, but it had never felt so important as now. One of the best and fastest sappers on the team, the others were depending on him like never before. His burrowing up to the surface could not be detected by the guards. Otherwise, nine months of labor and heartache would have been for nothing. Worse still, it might result in some of them being shot. Kit in one hand, candle in the other, he squirmed through the tunnel. The first stretch, with its downward slope, was easy going. He knew every turn, dip, hollow, and rise by heart. He knew when to duck his head and when to worm sideways to avoid a protruding stone. He continued to pray as he went.

At the tunnel's end, he put his kit to the side. Sweat soaked his hair and collar. Without taking a break, he started digging straight upward. The trowel made easy work of the soft dirt and clay, which poured down on top of him—coating his hair, sticking in his eyes and ears, trickling down his neck. He paid no mind to the discomfort. The sooner he got to the surface, the more time they would all have to get away. What was more, any delay meant that fewer officers in the ruck would be able to escape as well. Within a half hour, he reached the surface and took his first breath of fresh free air. Rain pelted down, and the light from the camp arc lamps looked unnaturally bright. His hole was only six inches in diameter, but it was a start. He dug faster now that he could kneel up in the tunnel and extend his arm, faster too no doubt because freedom was within reach.

The next two officers on the list, Andrew Clouston and William Langran, joined him after a half hour, as planned, and the two of them packed the earth piling up around Butler into the offshoot chamber. By 11:40, the hole was wide enough to climb through to the surface. First, Butler pushed his kit up out of the tunnel into the field. Then, using his arms and feet to brace the sides of the six-foot-deep hole, he slowly rose. His hair was soaked, and rain mixed with dirt poured down his grimy face. As he eased his head overground, he was pleased to discover that the exit came out beyond the first two rows of beans. He climbed up into the field and crawled on his belly to where the bean plants started. Hiding amid the dense leaves, he searched for the guard stationed outside the prison wall. The arc lamps and the shadows they cast made it hard to see. For all he knew, the guard might be standing still, eyes fixed on the tunnel exit because he had spotted some kind of movement there. Then the guard coughed, and Butler saw him at last against the darkness of the wall. He was pacing to and fro, obviously unconcerned and unalarmed. In that moment, the rain halted, the clouds overhead gave way, and moonlight shone down on the field.

Holzminden from the outside, with fields in foreground.

Minutes before the rain stopped, Private Ernest Collinson, an Army Service Corp driver and one of the orderlies, had been staring at the bean rows from the first-floor window of Block B's orderly quarters. For over half an hour he had searched through the darkness for any sign of Butler. He should have cut through to the surface by now. Perhaps, Collinson thought, he had missed him because of the lights and the sheeting rain. He might already be in the rye field or on his way to the Weser, but he had no way of knowing for sure. And Gray and his team needed to know definitively that Butler had made it out before they proceeded into the tunnel themselves. They were depending on Collinson to tell them.

Gradually, the moon broke through the clouds. There, amid the bean rows, Collinson spotted a hunched figure. In the next moment, the man crawled toward the stalks of rye, followed soon after by two others. Collinson hurried from his observation post to the stairwell. In his socks, he barely made a sound. Once up on the attic floor, he clambered through the small door, quickly crossed the eaves, and knocked on the panel into the officers' quarters. Grieve pulled it aside. "Butler made it," Collinson said. Little else was needed. The next batch of tunnelers—including Blain, Kennard, and Gray—filed into the eaves. Collinson followed them back into the orderly quarters. When he offered to lead them down to the cellars, Kennard said, "Don't bother, Collinson, we'll see ourselves out."

CHAPTER 17

"Chocks away," Blain said, tossing his kit ahead of him into the hole, but the bravado he had maintained throughout the evening quickly dissipated as he crawled in after it. Kennard followed, then Gray. Those who had gone before had left a few tin-can lamps burning along the path, but, given the passage's many kinks and turns, the three crawled mostly in pitch darkness. They did not want to waste time by holding candles. Blain kept up a good pace, pushing his rucksack ahead of him. He wriggled a few inches on his elbows. Pushed the rucksack. Wriggled. Pushed. When his jacket caught on a rock or when he slowed to take a breath, he felt Kennard's bag push up against his feet.

During one stretch, which was lit by candlelight, Blain suddenly found himself staring straight into the face of a rat. Its eyes were like black beads. He had seen many rodents while working in the tunnel, but the sight still sent a shiver down his spine. Before he could brush it away, the rat disappeared into the darkness, its senses no doubt alive to an exit ahead. The tunnel had never felt so long nor looked so ominous. Blain found himself panting for breath, and his arms grew heavy from pushing his kit ahead of him. The shadows cast about the narrow, misshapen bore resembled monsters awaiting to attack. He wanted nothing more than to be free of it. Then he saw a light up ahead, shining

ZMINDEN TUNNEL. JUL

The entrance to the Holzminden tunnel, July 1918.

down into the tunnel. He panicked. The Germans must have found the sap exit. They were lost.

He would have scrambled away had there been anywhere to go. Instead, he lay flat and motionless as a stone. "What's up?" Kennard asked, his voice little more than a muffled mutter. His claustrophobia was making him more anxious than ever. Blain angled his head to the side, his eyes adjusting enough to see that the light was simply the glare of the arc lamps through the hole. But he now found himself stuck. Gray added his muffled demand to know what the problem was. Kennard thumped the back of Blain's boots. Finally, the young pilot wrenched free and moved ahead again, his heart beating like a drum in his chest. After a couple more feet of crawling, he reached the tunnel exit and breathed a cool draft of fresh air. He rose to his knees, then to his feet, in what he figured might well become his vertical grave. Only the encouragement from Kennard and Gray kept him moving. He eased his kit out into the field, then squirmed himself upward. As his head rose out of the tunnel, he fully expected to hear the crack of a gunshot. When he was met only by the patter of raindrops, Blain finally caught his breath and calmed down.

Sixty yards away, Holzminden was cast in a ghostly white pallor by the arc lamps swinging in the wind. The guard paced back and forth by the wall, his rifle tucked under his arm, his coat collar tight around his neck. The wind blew from the southwest, stealing away any sound Blain might make. Taking care anyway, he eased himself slowly up into the field and kept his body low as he scrambled through the rows of beans. Then he stopped and looked back toward the tunnel exit. Kennard, then Gray, then the others behind them emerged in close succession. It looked like their heads and feet were connected, and they resembled a huge, mud-splattered crocodile. Blain almost laughed at the spectacle.

At last he reached the rye field. Some of the fallen stalks rustled loudly underfoot. Afraid that the guard would hear the racket, he waited at the edge of the field for Gray and Kennard to catch up. In whispers, they debated advancing into the rye versus crawling along the edge of the field until they were far enough away from the camp. Taking charge, Gray decided to go through the stalks. It was the quickest way, and he was sure that the rainfall would deaden any noise. They crunched their way into the field, Blain convinced that the guard would hear them and that cries of alarm were bound to follow—no doubt with dogs soon after. When nothing happened, he relaxed enough to straighten up from his crouched walk and speed up. After the rye field, they came to the main road that ran between Holzminden and Arholzen, the nearest town to the northwest. They knew from their German accomplices that during the night the police patrolled this stretch of road on bicycles, and they were sure to wait until they were confident that the coast was clear. Then Gray led them northward through more fields of rye and corn, to the top of a low hill.

There they dropped their rucksacks to the ground and took a brief rest. In the distance, the town of Holzminden seemed to float in a sea of darkness. At last, they were able to savor their freedom. They were masters of their own fate again. The air never tasted fresher; the hunk of Caley's Marching Chocolate never sweeter. "Bet Niemeyer wouldn't be sleeping so well if he knew where we were," Blain said.

"Let's hope nothing disturbs his slumbers until morning," Kennard replied.

"Just let's make sure," Gray said, "we never see that bastard again." They let the thought linger, then tramped down the hill to the Weser. The river served as a natural barrier to any escape westward. Bridges over it were patrolled, and its fast, deep waters had delayed—or altogether foiled—earlier escape bids. They needed to cross to its opposite bank before first light of dawn, at roughly 4:30 a.m. Otherwise, they were sure to be recaptured.

Charles Rathborne thrust his body into the tunnel, the fit almost as tight as a cork being pushed into a bottle. The already stout officer had been made stouter by the two suits he wore: one to get dirty and be thrown away, the other his disguise—a German civilian on a cross-country train journey. He had only been down into the sap once before and had never gone through its full length. He was quite unaccustomed to the claustrophobic environment and the effort it took to crawl through. The fact that his face was almost level with the dirt floor only deepened his discomfort. Nonetheless, he kept pushing himself forward, grunting and sweating as he went. Jim Bennett was behind him, like a race horse behind a mule, but there was no way around the senior officer, nor could he do anything about the walls and roof of the tunnel being disturbed by Rathborne's movement.

Rathborne was not the first to disturb the already shaky structural integrity of the tunnel. What with their kits and their eagerness to reach the exit, the officers of the first group of 13 who had gone before had knocked out struts, loosened rocks, and left chunks of dirt (as well as tins of food fallen from their rucksacks) along the path. Once the ruck arrived, the state of the tunnel would surely deteriorate further. After over an hour in the tunnel, Rathborne finally squirmed free. Stretched out in the bean rows he was certain he could hear the sentry breathing.

Bennett rose from the sap after him, followed by fellow airman Peter Campbell-Martin. They wished each other well, then Rathborne wriggled on his belly into the rye stalks. Once deep inside the field, he lifted up to his hands and knees and continued at a crawl. Beyond the rye field was one of corn. Such was the denseness of its narrow rows that he almost felt trapped by the crop. At last he broke free. He crossed a cabbage field, then brazenly hiked along the road that led south from Holzminden. While the others were headed west, in the direction Niemeyer would immediately suspect and send his guards, Rathborne had decided to go the opposite way. He planned to catch a train, the first of several, in Göttingen, 35 miles to the southeast.

Bennett and Campbell-Martin threaded 300 yards through the same rye and cornfields as Rathborne, albeit traveling much more quickly and in the opposite direction. They may have been moving in the direction Niemeyer would suspect, but they intended to do so at such a pace that nobody would catch up with them.

In Block B, Durnford was making his rounds, peeking into rooms, whispering to members of the ruck when they could start their escape now that the core team of tunnelers were out. At 12:45 p.m., he knocked on the door of Major Jack Morrogh of the Royal Irish Regiment, number 22 on the list. "Your turn, Major, and God bless you," Durnford said. Morrogh thanked him and rushed up the two flights of stairs to the attic. In the attic room, Grieve told him he would have to wait a bit longer. Someone was stuck in the tunnel. Morrogh hunkered down beside the dormer window, listening to the gale and intermittent rain. Now and again, he looked out the window to watch the German guards on their rounds. Little did the one stationed outside the wall know that there were men several feet directly underneath him.

"All clear," an orderly announced from the eaves. Grieve allowed Morrogh and several other officers to pass. They crept along the length of the barracks through the eaves, down the stairs, and into the chamber. After shaking hands with a fellow Irishman, Corporal Mackay, Morrogh entered the tunnel. It was the first time he had ever been in it. Following a quick descent of the initial slope, he found himself in pitch black. The tightness did not surprise him as much as the roar of sound. The long snake of men ahead of him—their heavy breathing, wriggling bodies, clanging kit bags, and curses—made for an almighty din. The guard aboveground must be able to hear them for sure.

He inched forward, wrestling past broken struts and piles of dirt and stone. The tunnel was in a sorrowful shape. Just as he began to gather some kind of rhythm, using his grip on his rucksack to pull himself forward, he felt like he hit a wall. Then the wall started to back itself up against him. The man in front was attempting to reverse. Morrogh tried to shout at him, but with his face inches from the damp earth, his voice came out muffled. Stuck and panicking, the man in front thrashed about, kicking his legs and twisting back and forth. Meanwhile, the officer behind Morrogh pushed at his heels. Crushed between the two, Morrogh was terrified. At last, the man ahead jerked himself free, moved on, and Morrogh was able to start crawling again. He was tired, desperate for fresh air, and harried by the continuous noise.

He managed only a few feet before he encountered a large stone blocking his path. The officer in front must have dislodged it in his panic. Using his rucksack, Morrogh shoved the stone a few inches forward, hoping to find the place on the tunnel's wall where it had broken loose. If it had fallen from the roof, there would be no hope. Bracing his legs, he thrust against the stone. Then again. Then again. He was damaging the sides of the tunnel, but he had no choice. Feeling with his hands, he found the place where the rock had come off the wall. With one last shove, he returned it to its place. The tunnel was disintegrating with the ruck's every movement. Morrogh feared he might never find his way out.

CHAPTER 18

David Gray scanned the river for the narrowest point to cross. The storm had roiled the black waters, and the distance to the opposite shore looked like an ocean. Kennard was scouting the banks and spotted a dilapidated fence bordering a nearby field. He had an idea and started breaking off slats. Bound together, the wood could serve as a raft for their clothes and rucksacks. By the time he and Blain had gathered enough wood, Gray had found a point to begin their swim. It would still be at least 150 yards across to the other bank. They stripped down to their underwear, bound up their clothes, and put everything on the roped-together fence slats. Their watches read 2:15 A.M.— before they too went into the rucksacks.

The men were already soaked through by the rain when they slipped into the tepid water. The shifting clouds overhead cast the river alternately in darkness and moonlight. Fearing a patrol, they waited for it to be dark before pushing away from the bank. They swam furiously for the other side, each holding on to a side of the raft to keep it steady. Waves swept over their heads, and by the movement of the trees on the opposite shore, they could tell that the currents were dragging them swiftly downstream. On they went, kicking their legs and swinging their arms. Halfway across, they were already breathing heavily, their limbs weary. A whitecap almost pitched over their raft, but they managed to keep it afloat. Desperation and nothing else drove them to reach the western shore. At last, they climbed onto the bank and collapsed with relief. After recovering a little, they emptied the raft. The wind and rain chilled them to the bone as they put their damp clothes back on. Kennard dragged the raft a few hundred yards up the bank to throw off the German bloodhounds that were sure to follow on their trail.

Gray suggested they march as far north that night as possible, believing that the search area would concentrate on the forests west of the Weser. Blain and Kennard agreed. At first, they followed the road beside the river. Although it ran a serpentine course, Gray figured the extra distance on the road would be covered far faster than tramping a more direct line north through forests and muck-mired fields. Gray and Blain both carried heavy rucksacks containing their food stores and other key supplies. Kennard carried only their spare kit with extra clothing, tobacco, and chocolate in it. If they encountered any Germans, he would have to ditch it quickly before they saw. A madman on the run would not be expected to have prepared a bag.

They shed their pajamas outside the town of Heinsen and hid them in some reeds. The filthy clothes had done their job of keeping their outfits underneath clean. The small villages of Polle and Brevörde were empty as they walked down the main streets. A dog barked at their presence, but otherwise they passed through unnoticed. Dawn approaching, they walked a little farther before veering off the road into some thick woods to hide during the daylight hours. They were roughly nine miles from Holzminden, and nine miles would have to be enough.

They ate a light meal—a tin of ham and some black bread—and smoked cigarettes. Blain got a good chuckle out of the other two when he told them about how they and their fellow officers looked like a "huge crocodile" streaming out of the tunnel. He volunteered to take the first watch. Exhausted, Gray and Kennard agreed and went quickly to sleep. Blain stared out into the surrounding darkness of the woods and wondered how his fellow breakout artists were faring.

There was trouble in the tunnel. Lieutenant Edgar Garland, a pilot from New Zealand, was halfway through when the man in front of him stopped moving. Garland rattled his boot, but the officer did not react. Perhaps he had fainted. Garland had a flashlight, but its narrow beam did not penetrate far in the twisting burrow. "What's the idea?" he shouted. "Having a rest?" "The tunnel has fallen in, and they are trying to clear it," the man in front called back. "It will only take a few minutes."

Garland rested his head down in the dirt and tried to calm his breathing. The air was bad from all the men down in the hole. If there was a block, it was sure to get worse. Moments later, he felt someone jamming up against his feet. The chain of officers behind had caught up. "What's wrong?" a voice at his feet gasped. Garland explained, confident that the block would loosen and that he would still make his home run to Holland. He was too confident.

The sap had caved in completely, several feet shy of the exit. Twenty-nine officers had made it through, including Jack Morrogh, but now dirt and stone had cascaded down the slope and rendered it impassable. Major Marcus Hartigan, a 38-year-old veteran of the Boer War and next in line to break out, only just managed to scramble backward before being buried alive. Try as he did to reopen the face of the hole with his hands, there was too much earth blocking his path. If they were to survive, then the men behind him—a dozen in all—needed to abandon their escape and crawl back out of the tunnel before the oxygen ran out.

Back at the sap's midway point, Garland waited. Fifteen minutes. Then half an hour. Nobody was moving, and, from the gurgling sound echoing through the sap, the men were starving for oxygen. With his own arms weakening, he was sure he was in the same boat. Now and again he flicked on his flashlight for some relief from the inky darkness. Thoughts of dying came to him. He had almost lost hope when the officer behind him said that he was headed back. Garland followed, hauling his rucksack behind him. Time and again, the retreat halted. The men were sapped of strength, and their coats and kits kept snagging on rocks. At last, Garland reached the slope that ran back up to the tunnel entrance. He might as well have tried to climb a cliff backward. Then someone grabbed his legs and pulled him out.

Alerted to the cave-in, Durnford and Grieve had organized a chain of men to haul out bodies. Their first concern was to get everybody out alive. Their second was to do so before 6 A.M., an hour fast approaching, when a guard would unlock the doors and send the orderlies out on their duties. If they failed to clear the sap, and if men were still moving about the orderly quarters, they risked the breakout being discovered long before the morning roll call at 9 a.m. Those three hours could prove the difference between escape or recapture for those who had made it out.

Some in the ruck had fainted or were too weak to evacuate the tunnel on their own. Garland volunteered to help drag them out. With great effort and at risk of falling victim to another collapse, he crawled deep into the tunnel again and managed to muscle one officer after another back through the hole. Shortly before 6 a.m., he had helped out all but Major Hartigan and the officer behind him. He remained in the chamber with a few others while the orderlies and officers sneaked back to their rooms and removed any signs of their nighttime activity.

Durnford watched from the windows for any hint that the breakout had been discovered, but the guards continued to walk their normal rounds. They might yet make it to the first roll call without any alarm. A half hour later, they had succeeded in extracting Hartigan and the other officer. Neither was in great shape, but they were still breathing. While they recovered, Garland and the others crept back up the stairwell, across the eaves, and into their own quarters.

Soon after, Hartigan and the other officer came straight out of the orderly door to Block B. They should have returned to their rooms through the attic, as the others had done, but they were too addled and oxygen-starved to think clearly. As they crossed to the cookhouse, they were seized by guards. Officers were not allowed onto the parade ground before 7 A.M., and certainly not officers exiting the orderly quarters in muddy clothes. Minutes later, Niemeyer stormed up and demanded to know what they were doing—clearly not having yet divined the reason. Neither answered. The standoff was interrupted by someone hammering on the eastern gate. A red-faced and clearly incensed farmer explained that a parade of men had stamped about his fields, ruining his crops. Niemeyer and his guards followed the farmer out of the gate and found the hole between the rows of beans.

"So, a tunnel!" Niemeyer exclaimed. He turned to one of his lieutenants, a man called Mandelbrat, and ordered him to find out how many had escaped. While Mandelbrat headed for the barracks, Niemeyer ordered another guard to climb down into the tunnel. The guard eyed the gaping hole, then his commandant, then shook his head. There might still be officers in the sap, he said. Next Niemeyer tried to send down his dog, but the animal balked at the order too. Niemeyer strode off to the Kommandantur. He rang the local police, the town's garrison commander, and, finally, General Hänisch in Hanover. A manhunt needed to be launched. No effort to be spared.

Mandelbrat had never cared much for Commandant Niemeyer and his constant derision, and, as he went about the corridors counting the men, he could barely suppress a thin smile as silence met his calling out the name of one officer after another. Murmurs of excitement followed him around the barracks. "The tunnel

German guards discovering the tunnel.

has gone, boys," one officer crowed to his roommates. A grand escape had indeed come off, and the only question was how many had managed to get away. Mandelbrat finished his count and went to join Niemeyer in the Spielplatz. *"Neun und zwanzig,* Herr Captain."

Durnford watched from the window for a reaction to the number he already knew. He described the moment: "Niemeyer's jaw dropped, his moustachios for a brief instant lost their twirl, his solid stomach swelled less impressively against his overcoat. Just for a moment he became grey and looked very old. But only for a moment." Then the commandant went beet red. He cursed and kicked the ground and shook his fists at the officers watching him from the windows, ordering his guards to shoot at anyone who appeared at the glass. Several shots were fired, but, used to Niemeyer's rages, the officers in the crosshairs had already dived to the floor. Throughout the barracks, the officers repeated the number like it had some kind of hallowed meaning. "Twenty-nine! Twenty-nine!" It was the greatest breakout of the war—the greatest, perhaps, in the history of warfare.

CHAPTER 19

Hunkered in corn stalks, Jim Bennett listened to the distant voices from a search party and the barking of their dogs as they scoured the woods a quarter mile away. Now and again, they drew closer to the field where he hid with Campbell-Martin. A couple of horse-drawn carts carrying soldiers also passed on the nearby road.

The escaped officers did not dare move during daylight hours. The hunt was intensifying, and, from previous experience, they knew that the German army would have informed the surrounding villages about the escape so civilians could join in the search with the police and military. Unless they put many miles between them and Holzminden, and soon, the net would only tighten. Still they remained in the fields, nervous and unable to sleep.

Only when it was well after dark did they continue, moving through the forest as quietly as they could. It was a starless night, and they had trouble maintaining their compass course. They soon found themselves lost in a gully, forced to backtrack through the dark woods until they found the right path again. Just then, they spotted what they thought was a German soldier. They were trying to creep around him when he called out in English. It was Philip "Murphy" Smith, a 22-year-old Irish cavalry officer and member of the ruck. They greeted each other and continued on together.

The small group started to head for Hummersen, down a road bordered by thick forests, when two men suddenly emerged from the trees in front of them: RNAS pilots Frederick Mardock and Colin Laurence. They informed them that Major Morrogh was a short distance away as well. When he caught up with them, they numbered seven. The area was clearly alive with escaped prisoners. The men sat down together in the woods to take a break. Morrogh regaled them with some of his adventures of the past few hours, including accidentally setting his entire tin of matches on fire, almost being found by a woman and her two children who were foraging in the woods where he lay naked while his clothes dried, and sleepwalking. He had woken up in the middle of the afternoon standing in a clearing, in "full view of anyone who might be there." His fellow officers laughed at these stories and had their own to tell too. Their voices and laughter grew louder and louder, and billows of cigarette smoke rose up from their huddle. Concerned, Morrogh put an end to the gathering. It was too dangerous to travel in such a large pack, they decided, so the men split off from one another. They needed to put as much distance between themselves and Holzminden as possible.

Kit bags over their shoulders, Gray, Kennard, and Blain threaded their way through the dark, dense forest. They kept to single file, ears keen for any sound other than the call of night birds or the skitter of a squirrel through the underbrush. In his many years in the military, Gray had become a skilled orienteer, and his steady compass bearings saved them from the many misdirections and lost time suffered by their fellow fugitives.

The three had started that day's march before dusk, balancing the risk of being seen against the benefits of getting beyond the 10-mile radius where they expected Niemeyer to concentrate his manhunt during its first 24 hours. They followed the roads where they could, but these tended not to be straight—and often led them toward hamlets or towns that they needed to avoid. Shortly after midnight, they reached Gellersen, roughly 15 miles from Holzminden.

On the outskirts of the village, a farmer spotted the trio, too late for them to turn back, hurry into a field, or find cover. They continued, hoping that Gellersen's main street would be abandoned at that hour, as the other villages they had passed that night had been. To their surprise, they found the opposite was true: Oil lamps flickered in many of the windows, and huddles of villagers stood outside their cottages, clearly disturbed. The three British airmen were sure that news of the Holzminden escape had reached Gellersen and that the villagers were stirred by the potential of the enemy loose in their area. It was time to see if Gray's scheme would fool anyone. Before reaching the first house, Kennard slipped his kit bag to Blain. Then Blain and Gray bookended Kennard, each putting a hand on his arm like they would if he were actually an asylum patient who might bolt off at any second. Occasionally Kennard tried to pull away from their grasp, and his two minders wrenched him back in line.

Gray did not slow his pace or hesitate as they advanced down the street. Unless they were stopped, he did not intend to explain their presence. He was on official business, with the papers to back him up. Conversations halted, and they felt every eye on them as they passed. Whispers followed in their wake, and a parade of villagers trailed after them. There would be a confrontation for sure, but the closer they were to the far side of town, the better it would be for them if they had to make a run for it. All the time, Kennard struggled against the grip on his arms, occasionally rolling his eyes for good measure.

When they reached the last cottage, a few villagers crossed over into their path and blocked their way. They stopped, and Gray drew his papers out from his pocket: his identity card, in the name of Franz Vogel, and the letter stating his duties as chief guard at the Vechta insane asylum. He told them in fluent German how the madman Kurt Grau had recently absconded from the asylum. Tilting his head in the direction of his increasingly agitated charge, he added that he recommended they give them a wide berth. This had some effect on the villagers, but not enough for Gray. His charge was prone to convulsions, he said, and it looked and sounded like one was coming on. He requested some water, so that they could give him "a quietening drug," to calm him down. On cue, Kennard tried to break loose, a low growl rising from his throat. Blain grabbed his arm and knocked him roughly on the side of the head. Gasps of shock rose from the villagers, and one ran off to fetch some water. Feeding on the reaction, Kennard whimpered and shook like he had no control of his limbs. Seemingly immune to his antics, Gray informed anyone listening that they could only travel by night since encounters such as these only set the lunatic off.

When a villager brought a glass of water, Blain put his hand out, stopping him. He leaned over to Gray and whispered. "No glass," Gray explained. Grau might break it and use the shards as a weapon. With that, they had the villagers completely fooled. A pewter mug of water was found while Kennard thrashed about like his tunic was on fire. They managed to wrestle him to the street, pinning him down by his arms and legs. He only fought harder until a pill was forced between his lips and washed down with the water. Sparing no drama, he writhed about. With every passing moment, he grew weaker, his twitches more spasmodic. At last he grew still.

The villagers were in a state of shock, but Gray promised them that the patient would awaken in a short while, no worse off than he was before. During the wait, he and Blain enjoyed some wine, bread, and cheese donated by an elderly farmer, who clearly had taken seriously the request in the letter from Vechta's chief of police to give them "all possible help." They also gained some valuable intelligence: A manhunt was under way for some escaped POWs, and a company of soldiers was in the area. They were searching the countryside and guarding the road and railway line due north of Gellersen. When Kennard fluttered his eyelids awake, Gray and Blain helped him up off the street, then they led their groggy patient away from the town. Once clear, they celebrated their success, although Kennard lightheartedly bemoaned the clobbering he had received when they were forcing him down onto the ground. He was especially disappointed that his minders had not saved him so much as a crumb of the fresh bread.

By the morning of July 25, nobody from the breakout had been caught, and Niemeyer took out his anger on those who remained behind. He was furious when it was revealed that the tunnel entrance—the location of which was only discovered by digging up the entire length of the sap—had been right under the noses of his guards for months. His rage festered when crowds of Holzminden residents came up to the camp to see the great tunnel and to wonder aloud how it could have gone unnoticed. A photographer even appeared to take pictures of the scar of upturned earth that led from the field to the eastern entrance of Block B.

Niemeyer was obsessed with recapturing all 29 of the escapees. Such a mass escape would not only be an embarrassment to Germany, but no doubt more important to Niemeyer, ruinous to his career. As part of his campaign to find them, he even posted notices in local and national newspapers to ask for cooperation: "We urgently request help to get hold of all escaped officers in the interest of the defense of our country. We particularly call on the country populations, berry pickers, hay

The exit of the tunnel out into the field, after being excavated by the Germans.

collectors, youth military groups, hikers, and hunters to look out for anything suspicious. We know from experience that fugitives tend to hide in forests. At night one should watch out for any noise and especially the barking of dogs in villages. A high reward is promised for assistance." The reward offered was 5,000 marks—a substantial sum in war-torn Germany—for any information that led to the capture of a Holzminden prisoner, dead or alive.

On the afternoon of July 26, Rathborne arrived in Göttingen, a university town set on the river Leine. On his way into the town center, where he expected to find the train station, he came across a tavern. Although he did want to try out his disguise, his decision to enter was more on account of his parched throat. He figured that as long as he kept any conversation brief, nobody would realize that German was not his mother tongue. The tavern owner was an old woman who looked as much part of the place as the scuffed bar. When she slid him a bottle of beer without remarking on his accent or appearance, Rathborne was reassured that he could successfully pass himself off as German. He had drunk fine-quality drafts of beer in the past, in Berlin and in Munich, but no beer in his lifetime ever tasted better than the one that afternoon.

After leaving the tavern, Rathborne walked on, but without a map of the town he soon found himself lost in its tangle of streets, with their half-timbered houses and steepled churches. It would not do to ask for directions. Finally, he saw a sign pointing to the

rains from Holzminden. Times between 5 p.m. and 6 a.m. under
From Nov. 17 time table. Trains appear to be "through" to Aachn
have a through carraige as far as Coln.

Holzminden dep.	12.23	12.35	...	3.18	...	6.2	...	4.2	...	8.57
Soest arr.	3.20	3.50		6.11				6.41		1.18
dep. for M.	6.16	6.16		8.30				8.40		3.30
Munster arr.	8.3	8.3		10.39				10.11		5.3
Coln arr.	12.4	7.34		9.49		12.5		9.59		6.4
Aachen arr	10.15	10.35		11.37		2.31		11.34		7.59

Trains leave COLN principal station for MUNCHEN - GLADBACH 4
1.14 a.m. 6.16 p.m. 7.54 p.m. 9.38 p.m. Journey takes 2 hours exce
is a fast train. Re plan of AACHEN - A is the main station, but there is
traffic by the N of AACHEN.

A handwritten railway timetable for trains from Holzminden.

railway station and made his way there. The next train was not until 8 p.m. Not wanting to be seen loitering, he went back into town and bought a ticket for the cinema. The film was unmemorable, but the newsreel, which showed a macabre scene of the Kaiser's soldiers standing over the bodies of Allied soldiers—Rathborne's comrades—struck him to the core. The war had seemed at such a remove when he was in prison. Minutes before 8 p.m., he returned to the station and boarded his train. From his comfortable seat, he watched the fields and hills he had marched through that morning blend past outside his window.

- -

After their antics in Gellersen, Gray, Blain, and Kennard found a copse of trees and got some sleep. They had barely left the woods after sundown on July 25 when they spotted a company of soldiers and scrambled back into the trees to hide. The soldiers were so close the three officers could see their bootlaces as they passed. Gray learned from their conversation that another patrol had arrested an escaped prisoner farther down the road. There was nothing they could do to help him. After the soldiers were gone, Blain struck his lighter, and Gray examined the map. Every alteration of their route was laden with compromise: A longer distance weighed against a smaller risk of encountering another patrol; moving quickly along a road against the safer but more taxing option of a hike through the countryside. They decided to strike through some fields to circle around the soldiers and then across a well-hidden stretch of road. Then they marched on a northwestern course, sometimes cutting through farms and forested hillsides, other times keeping to the winding roads.

Every couple hours, they took a break and smoked a cigarette, hands cupped over the ends so the orange glow was not seen in the dark. At sunrise the next day, as they neared Hohenhausen, they had the advantage of some dense woods and so decided to hike on through the daylight hours. For the next two nights, much of the hours spent in a steady downpour, there were no main roads to follow. They took a yeoman's route, down country lanes and muddy paths, halting often when they saw soldiers and civilians—clearly part of the manhunt. They never stopped for any length of time, knowing well that a tracker or a bloodhound might be closing in on their trail. The patter of the rain was their only cover. Every blind turn down a track or into a gully left their breaths trapped in their throats. Their limited meals and constant thirst exhausted them, but the prospect of someone coming upon them at any moment without warning was even worse. The fewer confrontations they had, the better their odds. Their lunatic cover story might convince—or it might not.

As the bright red dawn of Sunday, July 28, was breaking, they reached the outskirts of Exter—only 36 miles from Holzminden. With the many cutbacks and looping roads, they had trekked much farther in their five nights on the run. They had still so far to go.

CHAPTER 20

For the next several days, Rathborne continued with his plan to crisscross Germany by train, taking third-class carriages on slow local trains that stopped in almost every town along the route. He knew that conductors and the police were much more rigorous in their inspections of express trains and better-class carriages than the ones he was on. A downside of third class, as well as the discomfort, was that it was full of chatty passengers with too much idle time. One young girl prattled away for their entire journey. Another time, a German soldier on leave from the front carried on and on about those nefarious Brits.

In Bebra, he went to rest outside the town, finding a spot in a stack of corn. After a late breakfast of beer, listening to the bitter complaining from his waitress about the shortage of potatoes, he returned to the station and headed on to Fulda. His train came in too late for him to go straight to Cologne, so he bought a ticket to Frankfurt. On arrival there, he cleared out of the station as quickly as he could to avoid any chance encounters with the authorities. His gray suit was dirty, but it was nothing compared to his white shirt, which was so soiled he might have spent the night in a coal mine. He stopped into a tailor's shop to replace it, but when asked what size he needed he could only stare blankly, then make a fast exit. He had no knowledge whatsoever of German collar sizes.

There was more trouble when he went to eat dinner at a restaurant. The garrulous owner remarked that he could not quite place Rathborne's accent. The British officer replied that he was Polish by birth—but he did not stay for dessert in case he was asked any more about his background. He spent the next couple hours in the cinema before it was time for his overnight train to Cologne. He slept fitfully on the 100-mile journey, coming into the station on Sunday morning. Cologne was in a sorrowful state. Most shops were shuttered, and those that were open—butchers, bakers, and grocers—had long lines snaking out the doors. The faces on the streets wore a forlorn gaze, and men, both young and old, hobbled past with war injuries. Concerned about his appearance, Rathborne visited a barber for a shave and a haircut. His next train—to Aachen, a spa town a mere five miles from the Dutch frontier—departed that evening. He spent the afternoon in parks, beer halls, and the cinema, having become an expert in whittling away the hours, seen but unseen, a travel-weary businessman who just wanted to get home.

At 9 p.m., two hours after his train rumbled out of Cologne, Rathborne arrived into Aachen. He hopped on a tram that terminated at the Ponttor, the medieval gateway northwest of the old city center. From there, he walked to the town outskirts. He had a meal and a glass of gin at a small bar, fortifying himself for the last leg of his escape. Then he hid out behind a railway embankment. With map and compass in hand, he charted a route to the border that stayed clear of any roads or villages. At 11:30 p.m., the sky completely dark, he stashed his valise by the embankment and started west. He had gone only a short distance and was walking through some cornfields when a steady rain started to fall. The pitter-patter masked the sound of the stalks crackling underfoot. For an hour he pushed his way through the crops.

All of a sudden a pack of dogs started barking. Rathborne dropped down and lay flat, sure that the dogs were close enough to sniff him out. When the dogs quieted, he heard the voices of soldiers. For a long while, he remained absolutely still as the rain soaked through his clothes, leaving his skin cold. Neither the barking nor the voices came any closer. He decided to move ahead. He crawled on his hands and knees, fallen corn stalks cutting his palms as he went. He heard soldiers now and again but decided that his best option was to continue. He was uncertain as to how far he had gone—with the dense stalks it was slow going. On he crawled, hoping the border would come before the sentries pounced. He had to be close . . .

On their own, or in bands of twos and threes, many of the escaped officers were recaptured and returned to Holzminden. Captain Frank Sharpe and Lieutenant Bernard Luscombe, numbers 28 and 29 out of the tunnel, were the first to come back through the gates. Niemeyer glowered at them as they passed. The two men had made little preparation and had only a slim head start before the tunnel was discovered. Soldiers nabbed them 15 miles downriver, on the banks of the Weser. With the return of each tunneler, the mood among the rest of the Holzminden prisoners darkened. Would not any manage the home run to Holland?

Although filthy and stinking, Sharpe and Luscombe were sent immediately to the cellars. No water to wash, no change of clothes was offered, and they were put on a bread and water diet. Niemeyer followed them down to solitary, in a venomous mood. He took Sharpe's gold watch and put it on the table. Using a knife, he stabbed and crushed the precious heirloom into pieces. Then he ordered the guard to tear the civilian outfits Sharpe and Luscombe were wearing into "ribbons." The two were left half-naked. Niemeyer gave strict orders that nobody was to communicate with them nor provide any additional food. As far as he cared, they could rot.

Others soon joined them. The police, soldiers, and bloodhounds sent out on the manhunt had less impact than the countless German citizens who had been summoned. Whether out of patriotism or greed for the reward, they were incredibly effective. Butler, the first out of the tunnel, was nabbed in a village after he stole a bicycle. Others were flushed out of fields or taken while lost at crossroads. By Monday, July 29, 10 of the 29 escapees had been returned to the camp. Their sorry state—grubby outfits, sallow faces, bodies wasted from loss of food—only darkened the mood further. Morale among the prisoners deflated. It looked like none of the fugitives would make it to Holland.

With each recapture, Niemeyer swelled in his blue greatcoat. Never one to let good fortune pass without boasting about his own hand in it, he invited in reporters to chronicle each one. They wrote down what Niemeyer dictated, with embellishments for color. Without exception, Niemeyer insisted, the prisoners only succeeded in their escapes because of British accomplices outside the camp. There was an army of spies in the vicinity, he claimed, with no end to their supplies of clothing, food, and intelligence.

Try as Niemeyer did to wring a confession from the captured escapees, not one of them admitted to even using the tunnel, let alone to having dug it. His attempts to befriend and bribe the orderlies, Cash included, to get them to spill on the conspiracy and on who was involved, also failed. Lieutenant Colonel Arthur Stokes-Roberts, senior officer since the departure of Rathborne, believed that the mass escape would surely see Niemeyer removed from his position. But when General Hänisch sent an officer to investigate the events, he made clear that Niemeyer would stay. No crime of war or level of incompetence seemed capable of dislodging that bully from power.

Niemeyer's inquiries and his abuse of the returned prisoners stirred the pot of rebellion throughout Holzminden. One day, the officers lit cigarettes and pipes at roll call, which was not allowed. A thick cloud of tobacco smoke billowed around the Spielplatz. Another day, they refused to answer their names at roll call. Another, they came out bare-chested. Each time, Niemeyer sent in his guards to herd them back into the barracks, each time with a little more violence. So many prisoners had been arrested for violations that they eventually had to be housed in the town jail.

By looking at where the escapees had been caught, Niemeyer had a bead on the remaining men's westward line of flight: Holzminden, Bodenwerder, Hamelin, Lohne, Bielefeld, Ahaus, Gronau, and on to the Dutch border. He focused his attention on seeing his fugitive prisoners returned, directing the search himself and calling for local assistance along that route. Even if the prisoners did find their way to the border, he knew well that they would be bedraggled and half-starved. The German sentries would find them easy picking—and his record might yet go unblemished. The easy capture of an exhausted Jack Morrogh by the Ems River was sign of this truth.

By early August, 15 prisoners were still on the run. But Holland was a long way off, and Niemeyer was confident that he would win out in the end. Then one day he received a random telegram sent from Holland. It was written by one Lieutenant Colonel Charles Rathborne. It said: "Having a lovely time [STOP] If I ever find you in London will break your neck [STOP]."

The first of the breakout artists had made it.

CHAPTER 21

Dogs were barking in the village of Twiehausen, but the surrounding fields were too thick with mud to allow Gray, Kennard, and Blain to circumvent the hamlet. Rain poured from the sky. They thought they wouldn't have any trouble passing unnoticed through the single lane of cottages in the middle of the night, but with every step they took, another dog howled in one of the cottages. They would have a better chance tiptoeing through a kennel with steaks around their necks. A few cottage doors opened, and villagers peered out to see what was causing the ruckus.

Earlier in their journey, they might have hurried ahead—or not risked going through the hamlet in the first place. But after more than a week without proper rest, hiking miles every day, sleeping outdoors, eating half rations, and wearing damp clothes, they were cavalier. At last, they cleared the village, the cacophony from the dogs fading into the distance. Nobody had stopped them that time, but the three knew well that it only took a single mistake—the misreading of a sign, a careless hiding spot, an inquisitive passerby—and all would be lost.

The next night, they trudged through the swamp that encircled much of Dümmer Lake, bedeviled by mosquitoes. By the time they reached dry land, they were covered in bites. It was almost dawn, on August 1, but they continued until they had gone around the town of Damme. Every one of their 11 miles hurt. At last they hid in some woods to rest, the afternoon sun blazing overhead. They barely grunted in conversation they were so hungry and tired. During their almost two years of captivity, they had all lost weight, but after the past eight days of strain, half rations, and limited water, they were like skeletons. Their clothes hung loose on their frames, their eyes stared listlessly, and they were all suffering from colds. Blain's cheeks were sunken; he looked twice his age.

After dusk, they pushed through their exhaustion and marched down the road to Vehs. Due south of their route was Osnabrück, where they had first banded together to escape. It felt like a lifetime ago. They covered 16 miles that night, but in their ambition stopped too late to find anywhere other than a narrow thicket of trees in which to hide. By their map, Gray determined that they were roughly 45 miles from Sellingen, the Dutch border town, and that they should make their cross to freedom in four nights. They had rations enough for only two. Determination would need to cover the rest.

The next 24 hours followed much the same. Sleep, then a long, slow trudge, one foot after another.

In the late hours of Saturday, August 3, near the hamlet of Wieste, the road took a sharp turn away from their steady northwestward course. They left its easy track for a tramp through a deep marsh, their boots sticking in the mud. The only sounds in the night were their grunts of exertion and the sucking sound of the mud taking hold of each step. They did not have the energy to speak.

Over a dozen miles after they began, they collapsed in some woods yet again before daybreak. They slept soundly. Then, once dusk settled over the countryside, they began yet another trek. They passed through cultivated farmland from time to time, but their efforts to forage from the fields yielded nothing. The best nourishment they found was some rotten turnips that turned the stomach and raw potatoes that were better for cracking teeth than eating. Before morning, they intended to cross a point where the Ems River and canal met. That swim alone was enough to occupy their fears.

Southwest of Blenheim, perched high in the branches of a tree, Jim Bennett watched German soldiers go in and out of a camp just 300 yards away. It was one thing to see the Dutch border on the map, quite another to see its exact location and surroundings and to determine the best place to cross. Armed sentries patrolled the 350-mile border between Germany and the Netherlands, but there was no high wall, no single line of defense. In some places, there were manmade earthen embankments; in others, a canal or road separated the two countries. Sometimes electrified fences or barbwire divided woods and open fields, and there were also stretches where it was impossible to know what country you were in until you saw a guard or sentry post. In many senses, the border's irregularity, often dictated by the terrain, was its own defense. The longer you spent looking for an undefended spot, the more likely you were to be caught by a roving patrol or a farmer who would be rewarded handsomely for your return.

Early that morning, Bennett and Campbell-Martin had taken cover in the tree's dense foliage. By observing the movements of the frontier sentries, they had a good idea of where the border line lay. They figured their best opportunity was where it ran through some nearby woods. The day passed interminably. There was nothing for them to do but watch the guard and try to forget how thirsty and hungry they were. They had eaten the last scraps of their food, and, connoisseurs of puddle water, were desperate for something fresh to drink. Late in the day, a storm settled over them, turning the sky black. Rain beat down through the leaves, and the thunder cracked and boomed in every direction. It was fairly dark, and they might have set out early, but then the clouds broke and the sun shone brightly again, so they waited in their perch until the sun set and night stole completely over the countryside.

The two men then dropped down to the ground, fixed their compass for southwest, and started off across the moor. Thoughts coursed through Bennett's head about what might prevent him reaching freedom—electrified fences, dogs, burly sentries—and he figured out how he would overcome each. Only a bullet would stop him setting foot in Holland before dawn the next day—and maybe not even that. When they reached the woods where they believed the border to be, they dropped to their hands and knees and continued at a crawl. The rain had done little to dampen the crackle of leaves and twigs. It seemed that the closer they got to where they thought the border was located, the more noise they made. A few minutes later, Bennett spotted the line of a barbwire fence. The border. One hundred yards away at the most.

A lone sentry stood between them and freedom. They straightened up and eased slowly forward through the trees, grabbing heavy branches and sticks in case it came to a struggle. As yet, they had not seen any dogs, nor had they heard barking. Then, all of a sudden, there was a rustle in the woods a short distance away. Bennett stopped cold, and Campbell-Martin drew up alongside him. For a long moment, the two waited. All was silent, but Bennett sensed someone in the darkness ahead—someone restless and on alert. He was sure of it. He advanced—there was no turning back now. He had only gone a few steps when he heard the distinct cocking of a rifle and the sound of its butt being brought quickly to its owner's shoulder.

"*Halt!*" a German sentry ordered.

Bennett and Campbell-Martin knew what they had to do. They barely gave each other a look before they charged straight through the trees at the sentry, their sticks at the ready. Their sudden movement shocked the soldier, and he stood frozen as Bennett swept past, running so fast he did not have the time, nor the need, to use his stick. Campbell-Martin followed close behind. They found a break in the barbwire fence and raced through it. "*Halt!*" the sentry shouted again. The crack of a rifle echoed behind as they charged headlong into Holland. The first shot, and the next, missed. They ran and ran until they splashed into the Dinkel River in free Holland. On the opposite bank, they collapsed and shook hands. Together, both at the same time, they said, "We've made it!"

CHAPTER 22

On the morning of August 5, hidden in a stretch of woods outside Lathen and beyond the Ems River, Gray, Kennard, and Blain had their last meal—some Horlicks tablets (a mix of dried milk, barley, and wheat). Other than a couple squares of chocolate each, they were completely out of food. To warm them, Blain served out the few ounces of cognac left in his flask. They had long since smoked their last cigarettes, but the spirits offered some relief before the rising chatter of birds in the trees signaled that it was time to sleep.

At twilight, Gray spread out the last remaining section of the map. This was reason enough to be encouraged. He sensed his partners' spirits needed bolstering—and maybe his own too. There were no major roads to cross and only a few small hamlets to circumvent along their path, almost due west. On the map, the amorphous form representing the Walchumer moor separated them from Holland, eight miles away. A single night's march and they would be across the line, enjoying a hearty breakfast. Or, if things went the other way, they might be shot trying to cross.

The three airmen soon fell into the maw of the Walchumer.

They trudged through its narrow channels, across islands of peat, and into hollows that were waist deep with fetid water. Every step was unsure, their boots almost always either in a stream or buried in sticky mud. They slipped and stumbled, floundered backward, sideways, every which way. Often it was impossible to move forward without leaning on one another—or asking for a hand or a yank on their rucksacks to loosen them from the moor's sucking grasp. Night crawlers slithered underneath their clothes, and clouds of insects swarmed around them. If the three had known more about the Walchumer, they would have circumvented its clutches for sure.

Hour after hour, they struggled through, never on a straight compass line. Rain pelted down, mixing with the sweat in their eyes, and the sky was black. After 14 nights of marching, the previous two on little more than nibbles of chocolate, their bodies had no reservoirs of strength to offer.

What kept them going? Many things. The shame, unwarranted though it was, of being shot down and captured. Imprisonment—in one camp after the next—months, years, stolen from their lives. The separation from their squadrons and their families. The narrow escapes. The recaptures. Solitary confinement, sometimes pushed to the brink of madness and death. Holzminden. Its petty annoyances, its waiting, its drumbeat of theft and deprivation. The endless hours of tunneling, the terror of the dark, the fear of collapse and suffocating in the bowels of the earth. All the setbacks and the stubborn effort. And Niemeyer. His venomous harangues, his never-ending abuses.

The thought of Niemeyer, of besting him, was reason enough to continue. Above all, they wanted to be free, to be masters of their own lives again, to simply take a walk where and when they pleased.

It was approaching 4 a.m. on August 6 when Gray spotted a string of faint lights ahead. There were no towns nearby to explain their presence. Unless they had trekked far off their line, these had to be arc lamps illuminating the border. The first blush of dawn would soon appear, and they needed to be across the frontier before then. They crept slowly through the moor, feeling the stir of danger enlivening their bodies. The rain muffled their movements, but they made sure not to cough or splash in the puddles underfoot. Soon they were close enough to see a high dyke and on top of it individual lamps hung on posts, each spaced roughly 200 yards apart. German sentries paced back and forth between the posts, silhouetted by the light.

They discovered that the dyke was a sloped wall of mud and grass roughly 12 feet high. Backs flat against it, hidden from the sentry patrolling above, they took a few minutes to calm themselves and to ease their breathing. Then they started to watch the guard's routine: how long it took him to walk from post to post; how long his eyes would be turned away from them; whether he made any pauses along the way. Unable to see beyond the embankment, they had to take on faith that it would be a continuation of the moor. Once "over the top," Gray whispered, they would have to run as fast as they could through the bog. Only the darkness would protect them.

The guard paced away from their position, and Kennard turned to climb the dyke first. Digging the toes of his boots into the wall, grasping some bunches of short grass in his hands, he made it a few feet up before slipping down. His next attempt had the same result, and for an instant they feared the embankment might be insurmountable. Then Gray had an idea. Bracing his back against the wall, he threaded his fingers together, palms up, and told Kennard to step into the hold. This he did, and, with a quick jerk, Gray launched him up against the embankment. Kennard gained some purchase, enough to get his feet on Gray's shoulders to stop himself sliding down. Suppressing a grunt as Kennard bore down on him, Gray cupped his hands together again and heaved Blain up in the same way. Blain then used Kennard as a ladder to clamber to the top of the embankment.

At that moment, the sentry turned and came back toward them. Blain pressed himself against the edge of the dyke wall, fingers clawed into the mud, trying to keep himself from tumbling backward. Kennard supported him as well, with Gray holding up the human ladder at the bottom on already-exhausted legs. The sentry turned again, passing close enough to kick gravel down on top of them, but Blain remained unseen. After a short countdown, fearing Gray might buckle at any second, Blain scrambled up onto the gravel track that ran along the top of the embankment. As the sentry distanced himself, Blain yanked Kennard up to his side. Now they had to get Gray up before the German turned.

Forming a chain, Blain at the top, grasping Kennard by the legs, they leaned over the embankment and reached for Gray. Desperate as he was to reach them, his boots slipped on the mud like it was slushy ice. Every attempt he made to mount the few feet he needed to grasp Kennard by the hand ended in a tumble down to the dank moor.

Gray spotted that the sentry was about to turn back in their direction. "Duck!" he warned. Blain and Kennard slithered off the gravel track and clung to the edge of the embankment. With every second that passed, their fingers were losing the strength they needed to keep their hold. Both kicked their boots into the wall for support only to create a tumble of mud that splashed into the puddles below. They were sure they were lost at that moment, but the sentry continued on his beat, and Blain and Kennard climbed back up onto the track.

Gray had one more idea. If it didn't work, they would have to go on without him. Kennard stretched down as Blain held tightly on to his legs. Gray tied together the straps of the two rucksacks (his own and the one Blain had left behind). "Catch!" he hissed. He burst up the wall, throwing the bundle up at the same time, holding its end tightly. Kennard grabbed the bundle and hauled Gray up the side of the wall. Blain heaved them both up onto the embankment. At last Gray scrambled to the top, and the three sat gasping on the track. They could go on together.

The trio had barely realized that they had been successful when they heard the sentry yelling and saw him start to come toward them. "Run!" Gray shouted. "Down the bank! Run!" They leaped over the side of the dyke, tumbling and sliding until they hit the bottom. Then they hurled themselves blindly out across the moor. Rifle shots rang out behind them followed by curses and shouts in German. But the sentry was aiming at shadows in the dark and missed. They rushed on across the uneven terrain until the sentry's threats faded behind them. Then they slowed, but kept moving until Gray was sure they were well out of range and far over the border.

He drew to a halt, and Blain and Kennard stopped beside him. "It's all over," Gray said, throwing an arm around each of their shoulders. "We've bloody well made it!" Together they yawped, leaped up and down, hollered, and splashed in the marshy moon like schoolchildren in a puddle. In all his young life, Blain had never experienced such joy; it overwhelmed him. Kennard felt the same. He sat down on some grass and ate the last sliver of chocolate, which he had saved to celebrate if they made their home run. Then he wept.

"That, dear friends and fellow lunatics, is the Dutch village of Sellingen," Gray said, looking northward at a halo of lights. Then he returned to his usual restrained self and rallied them to their feet. "Come on, then. Let's not waste time. There's a war on, you know."

Outside Sellingen, Blain, Kennard, and Gray surrendered to the first patrol they could find. The Dutch soldiers received the three of them as if they were honored guests and took them to the nearby town of Coevorden. Put up in top-class accommodation at the Hotel Van Wely, they ate, shed their filthy clothes, bathed and shaved, then collapsed into beds that must have felt like clouds. The next day, they telegrammed their families. The notes were spare but glorious. Kennard's read: "Escaped and arrived safely in Holland. Expect me home shortly—Caspar."

Three other Holzminden escapees, John Tullis, Stanley Purves, and Edward Leggatt—all RFC—joined them at the hotel the next day. The six had a photograph taken, wearing wooden clogs, together with the owner of the hotel. Although their faces were gaunt from malnutrition, they all wore the looks of conquering heroes. Soon after, the Dutch military escorted them by train to Enschede, where they idled for a week in quarantine, segregated from a large contingent of German deserters. Bennett and Campbell-Martin met them there soon after. Including Rathborne, who had already gone ahead to England, and Lieutenant John Keith Bousfield, 10 of the 29 who escaped Holzminden made it to Holland.

It was the greatest escape of the war. Secret cables from the British Consulate in Rotterdam informed London, where Lord Newton and officials in the War Office, Military

A signed photo of Blain, Gray, and Kennard after their escape, in the outfits they wore.

Intelligence, and the Air Ministry celebrated the triumph. Even before the escaped officers left the quarantine camp, brief reports about the tunnel escape were hitting newspapers across Europe and in the United States. The *New York Times* headlined "British Prisoners Dig Out" but offered few details since the sensational nature of the breakout had yet to be fully revealed.

On the evening of August 15, the Holzminden escapees boarded a small ship in Rotterdam. They had new clothes, temporary passports, and a pocketful of money for their journey to London. As part of a large convoy escorted by destroyers, the ship pulled out of the Dutch harbor and traveled a circuitous route across the Channel. The following morning the officers were moved beyond words by the sight of the English shoreline.

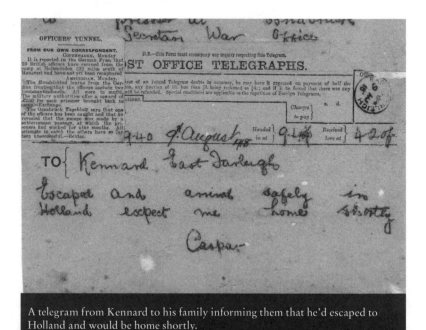

A telegram from Kennard to his family informing them that he'd escaped to Holland and would be home shortly.

They docked soon after in Gravesend. From the window of their train to London, Gray watched the countryside pass. It all looked as it always had: the rise and fall of fields bordered by hedges, cows lazing in the sun, towns tucked into hollows. Although he and the others had received updates about the war's progress, including the renewed Allied offensive that began only a week before, they still feared that their homeland had been ground down into a hopeless state—as German propaganda had promised for years now. Arriving at the station, they found the platforms crowded with young men in uniform. Outside, buses and taxis crammed the streets, and pedestrians thronged the sidewalks. Shops were open and restaurants bustling. To their quiet relief, Britain was alive and eager still.

Dispatched straight to the War Office, the men underwent a series of interviews, mostly run by the Intelligence Department, to learn about their experiences and what they had seen during their captivity in Germany. Gray delivered his report of prisoner abuses from earlier in the war. Then, as one escapee recorded, they were instructed to "take three months' leave and get fat." Before there was any meat on their bones, King George V invited them for a private audience at Windsor Palace, then sent a kind personal note to each officer. Blain's read as follows: "The Queen joins me in welcoming you on your release from the miseries and hardships, which you have endured with so much patience and courage. During these many months of trial, the early rescue of our gallant officers and men from the cruelties of their

Gray, Leggatt, Purves, Kennard, Blain, and Tullis after their escape to Holland, together with a Dutch police officer and the hotel owner.

captivity has been uppermost in our thoughts. We are thankful that this longed for day has arrived, and that back in the old Country you will be able once more to enjoy the happiness of a home and to see good days among those who anxiously look for your return."

As the tunnelers reunited with their families, reports of their breakout spread. Now that the details could be revealed, their exploits captivated the nation and the world. "The Tunnel to Freedom: British Officers' Escape from German Black Hole" said the headline in the *Daily Sketch*. "Daring Escape" echoed the *Evening Express*, in bold. With so much sacrifice and horror on every front, the Holzminden escape was a bright banner of hope—not to mention proof of British derring-do. The 10 men were put up for Military Cross medals.

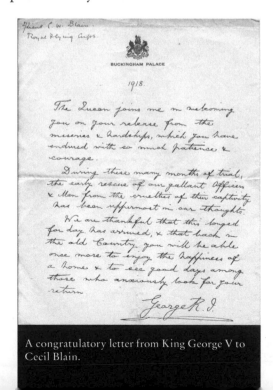

A congratulatory letter from King George V to Cecil Blain.

,060. Telephones: { London—Holborn 6512. / Manchester—City 6501.   LONDON, WEDNESDAY, DECEMBER 18, 1918.   [Registered as a Newspaper.]   ONE PENNY.

THE TUNNEL TO FREEDOM:

BRITISH OFFICERS' ESCAPE FROM GERMAN BLACK HOLE.

Right photograph showing the tunnel with the sandbags in which the earth acked. Biscuit tins, with the ends knocked out, formed an air shaft.

nnel after being dug up by order of the camp ties. The barracks, in the background, formed the prisoners' quarters.—(Exclusive.)

Capt. Niemeyer, the camp commandant, a "low brute."—(Exclusive.)

The black hole is the outlet of the original tunnel dug by Lieut. Ellis, R.F.C., who started the work nine months before the escape. The original tunnel was only just large enough to enable a man to wriggle through. The trench in foreground was dug up when the camp authorities had discovered the prisoners' escape and were making inquiries. —(Exclusive.)

photographs show how 29 British officers, including Lieut.-Col. Rathbone, tunnelled their way to freedom from captivity at Holzminden, one of the worst prison camps in any. With shovels and other implements they burrowed through a wall in the barracks basement and worked day and night by the light of tiny electric torches, till at they wriggled out. Of the 29 ten managed to reach Holland; the rest were recaptured. The camp commandant is one of the Hun brutes who must be brought to trial.

Despite all the attention that the Holzminden breakout artists got, most of them simply wanted to get back into the fight. As soon as their leaves were over, Gray and his fellow pilots Blain and Kennard returned to their duties. They had a war to win.

THE FINAL ROUTE OF BLAIN, KENNARD, AND GRAY, AS WELL AS RATHBORNE'S TRAIN JOURNEY

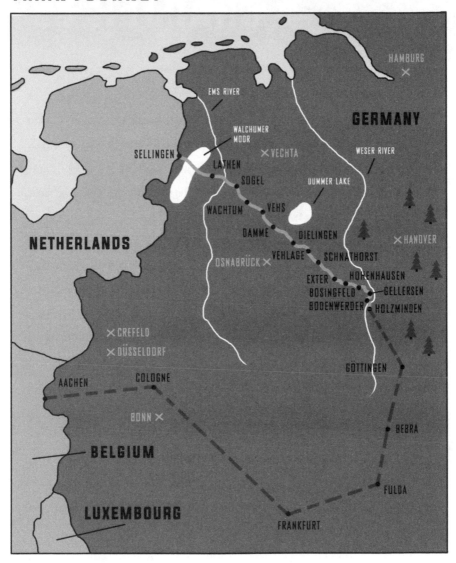

= The final route of Blain, Kennard and Gray
= Rathborne's Train Journey
• = Stops
✕ = Cities and POW Camps

CHAPTER 23

In the period after receiving Rathborne's telegram, Niemeyer seemed to go absolutely mad. Whether it was because of shame over the mass escape or too much drink, he became untethered. He raged at his charges like never before, accusing them of insurrection. He fired off his revolver into the air at the slightest provocation. He stabbed his cane at the laundry the prisoners hung from the wire fences—a sight that one officer likened to Don Quixote tilting his lance at windmills. Continued escape attempts, mostly by cutting the wire, only throttled up his temper even more.

As he had threatened to do, Niemeyer court-martialed the 19 recaptured prisoners. On September 27, officials from Berlin arrived at Holzminden to hold the trial there. The defendants were charged with mutiny and with "conspiring to destroy Imperial Government Property." Deciding that the indictment was a farce, some of the officers gave suitably farcical answers to questions about their name, rank, religion, and pre-war occupation. One declared himself a shepherd, others a diamond trader, a grammar-school pupil, a pensioner. The judges sentenced the lot to six months' solitary confinement in a prison fortress for "having made an escape by force with united forces." But with 250,000 American troops landing in France every month, Allied advances puncturing holes in the trench lines across the Western Front, mass desertions of German soldiers, and civil unrest in Berlin and elsewhere, the war promised to be over long before they had to serve even a fraction of that sentence. Negotiations for an armistice were already in the works.

Within days of the court-martial, Niemeyer suddenly turned into the prisoners' friend. He hired a photographer to come into Holzminden and made clumsy attempts to joke with the men and to gather them into happy groups for shots. "They would all be home for Christmas," he promised. No longer did he bluster around the yard, cock of the walk. He stayed mostly in the Kommandantur, inviting the senior British officer Stokes-Roberts to his office, approving most requests. Fewer roll calls, longer parole walks—whatever the men wanted. Niemeyer was aware that the British authorities knew all about his activities at Holzminden—Lord Newton having once demanded his removal—and he feared being tried for war crimes. When some prisoners warned him that justice would come calling, he claimed that he had "always done all he could for the officers and that if there had been any unpleasant orders, they came from above."

On November 11, the Armistice was announced, along with the news that Kaiser Wilhelm II had fled to the Netherlands, his rule over Germany at an end. Throughout the camp, portraits of the Kaiser disappeared. The prisoners tossed their caps in the air. They cheered and danced in the Spielplatz and removed the

German flag that flew from Block A. They freed those still in the solitary cells and drank and feasted and partied into the wee hours of the night. Neither the guards nor Niemeyer tried to stop them. In fact, Niemeyer immediately shed his uniform for a plain suit and declared to the camp, "You see, I am no longer a Prussian officer, but a Hanoverian gentleman." He had good reason to be worried: Socialist revolutionaries had already assassinated Hänisch. The following day, while the officers and orderlies at Holzminden wondered how and when they would return home, Niemeyer disappeared, no doubt with the riches he had extorted from them. Most of the guards fled as well. A company of German soldiers was sent to watch over the camp, but they largely allowed the men to do as they liked.

Dick Cash was one among many who used the new freedom to take walks into town. Holzminden's residents were in a desperate state, and they nearly rushed him when he presented packages of rice and tins of cocoa for trade. Many were starving, and the Spanish flu—a pandemic that would infect 500 million people worldwide—was beginning to claim lives.

Weeks passed without word of their fate, and the prisoners' supply of food soon dwindled down to potatoes and cabbages. The Germans handed out pamphlets sent from Berlin, entitled *A Parting Word*. They began, "The war is over! A little while—you will see your native land again." The propaganda promised a new Germany and concluded, "The valiant dead who once fought against each other have long been sleeping as comrades side by side in the same earth. May the living who once fought against each other labour as comrades side by side upon this self-same earth. That is the message with which we bid you farewell."

Yet this farewell did not come any closer. Eventually, Stokes-Roberts commandeered a train to take the Holzminden men west. On the night of their departure, December 10, they piled tables, boxes, chairs, trunks, old clothes, and anything else they could find that might be combustible into the Spielplatz and lit a huge bonfire. The German soldiers tried to extinguish the flames, but the British poked holes in their fire hoses. Framed by the glow of the blaze, they assembled into four columns and

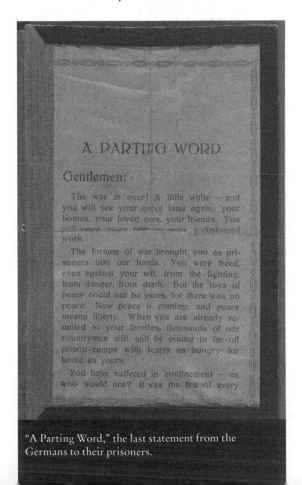

"A Parting Word," the last statement from the Germans to their prisoners.

marched out of the gates. In Holzminden town, the Germans lined the streets to watch them pass, a look of "awe, envy, and hate" on their faces, one officer wrote. The officers and orderlies boarded their train, making no separation for rank as they packed the carriages. With a jolt, they started down the rails, the bonfire at Holzminden growing fainter in the distance with each passing minute, until they could see it no more.

EPILOGUE

Twenty years after the Holzminden escape, on the evening of July 23, 1938, Lieutenant Colonel David Gray, commanding officer of the 48th Pioneers, headed down London's Fleet Street and ducked through the door of Ye Olde Cheshire Cheese, the pub that over the centuries had welcomed Sir Arthur Conan Doyle and Charles Dickens to drink under its dark vaulted ceilings. This night, it was hosting the twentieth anniversary of the Holzminden tunnel escape. Air Commodore Charles Rathborne chaired the dinner, and Jim Bennett was its organizer.

IT IS PROPOSED TO HOLD A

RE-UNION DINNER

on Saturday, 23rd July, 1938, at Ye
Olde Cheshire Cheese, Fleet Street,
London, to celebrate the 20th
anniversary of the

HOLZMINDEN TUNNEL

Air Commodore C. E. H. RATHBORNE,
C.B., D.S.O., will be in the Chair
and the Orderlies who helped in
the escape will be the Guests of
Honour. Lounge Suits—6.30 for 7
p.m. The Committee cordially invite
you to attend.

You will greatly assist by replying
AT ONCE to—

L. James Bennett, 39, Maddox Street, London, W.1

SUBSCRIPTION FROM OFFICERS 10/-

24TH JULY, 1918

HOLZMINDEN TUNNEL

20th Anniversary Dinner

at Ye Olde Cheshire Cheese, Fleet Street, London

23RD JULY 1938

Twentieth Anniversary dinner invitation and menu cover.

The surviving breakout artists at the twentieth anniversary celebration, examining items and pictures from the escape.

Sadly, Gray's two closest friends from that time were not there. In early 1919, Cecil Blain had crashed and died while test-piloting a Sopwith Dolphin for the RAF. He had been writing a memoir about the Holzminden escape. Gray was stationed in Russia at the time, fighting the Bolsheviks in the Russian civil war, and could not return for the funeral. King George V had sent his condolences to the Blain family, recalling the "gallant and able Officer" he had met only months before. So too did Gray miss the burial of Caspar Kennard. After the war, Kennard had gone home to Argentina, where he married and became the manager of large ranch. In 1935, he was killed in a freak shooting accident. "Kennard was a stout fellow, a good pal," his obituary concluded. "His untimely death will leave a feeling of great regret in the hearts of his fellow officers."

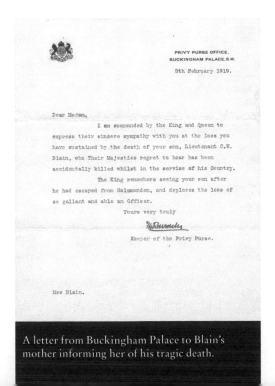

A letter from Buckingham Palace to Blain's mother informing her of his tragic death.

There were many others missing at the dinner, albeit because of distance rather than tragic circumstance. Dick Cash had returned to Australia to reunite with his family, and after the Armistice the Holzminden prisoners had spread out far and wide: from South Africa to New Zealand, to Singapore, India, Hong Kong, Barbados, Vancouver, and New York City. Those absent were recognized and remembered, but most of the evening was spent in laughter and conversation, recalling the moments both comic and horrifying they shared while tunneling to their freedom.

The breakout artists still wondered about the fate of Karl Niemeyer. At the Versailles Peace Conference it had been agreed that certain "enemy officers" should be brought to justice for their crimes. Niemeyer made the list, particularly after the death of William Leefe Robinson from the privations he had suffered at Holzminden. However, Niemeyer was never found. One report had him committing suicide in Hanover; others said that he had escaped to South America. Whatever the truth, perhaps the best laugh of the evening came when a mocked-up telegram from one of their fellow prisoners was delivered to the pub from Milwaukee, Wisconsin: "I know damn all about you and your dinner [Stop] Charles Niemeyer [Stop]." The roars of laughter from Gray and others were heard into the night.

Over the next few decades, the tunnelers and the other Holzminden prisoners—friends for life—would meet again for anniversaries. Gray, however, would not attend another of these dinners. When he had to leave the RAF in 1942, for reasons of age, he signed up for the Home Guard, a volunteer defense organization. That November, he died in a lorry accident—an inglorious end to an otherwise glorious and bravely led life.

David "Munshi" Gray, "The Father of the Tunnel," was buried with honors in Wonston, Hampshire. Most treasured among the items he left his wife, Violet, and their 19-year-old son were the escape kit, old maps, fake identification, and compass he had used in his home run from Holzminden POW camp.

The Holzminden escape had an impact far beyond those involved in its success. During World War II, Jim Bennett worked for MI9, a newly founded, top secret organization within British military intelligence, the purpose of which was to teach principles of evasion and escape to Allied soldiers, airmen, and naval personnel. For this, it called upon the first-hand experiences of those who had escaped the Germans in World War I, of which Bennett as a Holzminden breakout artist was an ideal example. Bennett usually began his talks by saying that becoming a POW was "improbable but possible." If taken prisoner, he advised the young men, "Your war effort is not finished." Each and every one of them had a duty to escape: Britain needed them back in its ranks, and an escape would absorb men and resources that might otherwise be used on the front line. They might suffer mental and physical deprivation, but they were to remember that their war effort was by no means done.

Bennett detailed escape routes from Germany and explained how to create a simple code for secret messages. He stressed the need to stay fit during captivity and the importance of having a compass in order to reach the border. Then he recounted his own experiences, his lack of preparation, the missed opportunities, the false starts, all before his final dash across the border. In his mistakes, and in those of his friends, there was much to learn. "Forewarned is forearmed," he liked to conclude.

Bennett played only a small part in the vast organization that coordinated escape and evasion across Europe and the Mediterranean, but he and his fellow breakout artists—Gray, Blain, Kennard, Rathborne, Leggatt, Medlicott, and so many others—were very much the inspiration for MI9 and its American counterpart, MIS-X. Their bravery and daring paved the way for their establishment. Given the Nazi penchant for torturing, and sometimes hanging, prisoners of war, these two organizations ended up saving many lives.

By one historian's estimate, there were 192,848 British and Empire POWs held in Germany during World War I. Among these, there were over 10,000 escape attempts, of which only 573 (54 officers, 519 other ranks) were successful. In contrast, before the collapse of Nazi Germany in 1945, 33,578 British, Commonwealth, and American POWs managed to return to Allied lines after finding themselves captured by the enemy. Some of the most daring escapes, including those from Colditz and Stalag Luft III, bear too many resemblances to the great escape from Holzminden to be a coincidence.

Bennett never spoke much about his captivity or escape. His family had no idea about his subsequent service in World War II until they found a dusty folder with papers that included his speech notes and travel receipts after his death in 1983 at the ripe age of 91. Instead, he focused his life on building a business, being a good friend, investing in a happy marriage, and raising a son and daughter. He was there to ensure that his children, Graham and Laurie, followed his version of the Golden Rule— "Do as you would be done by"—and to teach them how to ride a bicycle and drive a car. The opportunity to do so in freedom, in his own country, was reward enough for his contribution to the greatest escape of the Great War.

Bennett's lecture notes during World War II for Allied soldiers. His final words: "Escape as soon as possible."

COMING DOWN IN
ENEMY TERRITORY

CHOOSE A QUIET SPOT.

BURN ALL PAPERS AND PLANE

EVADE CAPTURE

NO LUCK

CAPTURE AND INTERROGATION

JOURNEY TO P.O.W. CAMP

LIFE AND CONSTITUTION OF CAMP

ESCAPE AS SOON
AS POSSIBLE

THE HOLZMINDEN ESCAPE LIST
JULY 23–24, 1918

SUCCEEDED IN HOME RUN

Jim Bennett

Cecil Blain

John Bousfield

Peter Campbell-Martin

David Gray

Caspar Kennard

Edward Leggatt

Stanley Purves

Charles Rathborne

John Tullis

RECAPTURED

Douglas Birch

Thomas Burrill

Walter Butler

Andrew Clouston

Frederick Illingworth

William Langran

Colin Laurence

Bernard Luscombe

Peter Lyon

Neil Macleod

Frederick Mardock

Arthur Morris

Jack Morrogh

Robert Paddison

Clifford Robertston

Frank Sharpe

Alan Shipwright

Philip Smith

David Wainright

SOURCES AND ACKNOWLEDGMENTS

Years ago, in a more adventuresome lifetime, I took some flying lessons with a fellow author (and experienced pilot) Tom Casey. I still vividly remember the exhilaration—and heart-dropping fear—of swooping over the coastline of Long Island, then around the tip of Manhattan, and up the Hudson River corridor. The experience sparked an interest in aviation, pursued more safely within the confines of histories of the same. My most avid reading focused on the early days of the Royal Flying Corps, and daring Oxbridge sorts who made up its early ranks of pilots flying their wood, cloth, and wire contraptions. Among those volumes that inspired further reading were H. A. Jones's magisterial *The War in the Air*, Cecil Lewis's *Sagittarius Rising*, and Denis Winter's *The First of the Few*.

Besides a hasty path to death, these pilots also faced a good chance of being shot down behind enemy lines, particularly as their activities ramped up in advance of the Battle of the Somme in 1916. Those who survived a crash landing were inevitably captured and imprisoned by the Germans. Rascals of the highest sort, many of these men attempted elaborate escapes that might well have been pulled straight from the pages of *Boy's Own* adventures. Only the incurious could then resist picking up one of what became an *oevre* of World War I breakout memoirs. They are too many to name, but among my early favorites were Gerald Knight's *Brother Bosch*, J. A. L. Caunter's *13 Days*, A. J. Evans's *Escaping Club*, and J. L. Hardy's *I Escape*. Time and again, these memoirs drew a line to what might best be described as the Alcatraz of Germany at the time: Holzminden.

I quickly fell under the spell of the classic *The Tunnelers of Holzminden* by H. G. Durnford, who played a bit part in the extraordinary events that led to the greatest breakout of the Great War. Upon consuming his memoir, I was sure I had my next book project in hand. That said, Durnford recounted the events—and characters of those involved—with the kind of emotionless British reserve that left me unsure of who these men were and what drove them. Then I came across the delightfully introspective, quirky, and beautifully written *Comrades in Captivity* by poet and Holzminden survivor F. W. Harvey. He put flesh and bone on what it was to be a prisoner in the archipelago of German camps and the desperation that pushed some to risk everything to be free.

All these books were inspiration—and great source material—but they were only the beginning on my journey to chronicle this narrative. One should always start with the low-hanging fruit, and I benefited from three earlier works on the Holzminden escape: *Beyond the Tumult* by Barry Winchester, *Escape from Germany* by Neil Hanson, and Jacqueline Cook's *The Real Great Escape*. Each in their own way provided excellent guidance, same as the holistic study of British POWs in Germany by John Lewis-Stempel in *The War Behind the War.*

Given these events occurred almost exactly a century before I started my research, I knew firsthand interviews were out, and I would need to depend on a rich and diverse range of primary documents. Fortunately, I struck gold early and often over the course of the project thanks to the wonderful archivists at the Imperial War Museum, RAF Museum, the British National Archives at Kew (a treasure almost unparalleled), the Bundesarchiv, and the Liddle Collection at the University of Leeds. They provided unpublished memoirs, oral history interviews, repatriated POW reports, letters, maps, and even artifacts from the escape by many of the key participants in these extraordinary events. Of particular note was a handwritten memoir by Cecil Blain at the Imperial War Museum. My front-line researcher for many of these finds was Claire Barrett. At the time, she was studying for her master's in the History of War from King's College, London. She proved tenacious and a quick study, and I owe a great debt to her for following up my leads—and generating quite a few on her own. In a word, she is top-notch. Thanks also to early research by Norma Bulman and Allmut Schoenfeld.

I would also like to make a special callout to the F. W. Harvey Collection at the Gloucestershire Archives. They hold an absolute treasure trove of letters, scrapbooks, personal documents, notebooks, and other papers from the soldier-poet. If nothing else from this book, I am proud to have played a part in resurrecting the memoir of this incredible individual. I was ably assisted in accessing this collection by James Grant Repshire and Steve Cooper, representatives both from the F. W. Harvey Society. Thank you also to Mrs. Elaine Jackson of the Harvey family who gave me permission to quote from the collection. It is truly a window into the soul of these heroes.

Where archives came up short, I depended on the kindness and generosity of the families of many of the principal individuals in this escape. After so many years, some were a challenge to track down across the world (online family trees and Facebook are a researcher's new best friend!), but perseverance paid off in spades. Much of the incredible story of Royal Navy Air Service observer Leonard James Bennett had been lost to history, but thanks to his daughter Laurie Vaughan, I had access to his unpublished memoirs, notes from lectures, and page after page of letters he sent from Holzminden during his captivity. More important in some ways, Bennett verified the link between the breakout artists of World War I with the founding of MI9, the British escape and evasion service that saved so many lives during World War II. I would also like to thank Laurie's granddaughter, Lily Peschardt, who collected many of these writings in her graduate school project Home This Afternoon.

Many other families assisted with letters, unpublished memoirs, photos, and other bits of information. This book could not have been written without them. Thanks especially to Hugh Lowe, Brian Tullis, Keil Tullis, Brenda Merriman, Pete Clouston, Jane Gray, Diana Gillyatt, Kit Kennard, Margaret Pretorius,

Mal Lyon, Tony Wheatley, and Julyan Peard. Although I could not tell each prisoner's story in full, I hope the families know how instrumental their efforts were. Thank you also to Jacqueline Mallahan for her generosity in sharing her late husband Patrick's vast archival collection and research into the RFC and POWs in World War I.

Despite such a huge number of sources, there remained some mysteries, particularly as to the arrival and departure times of some of the prisoners to Holzminden—and their specific activities in the early foundation of the tunnel. The tremendous archive/tracking service of World War I POWs collected by the International Committee of the Red Cross was invaluable in solving some, but not all, of the prisoners' movements in and out of camps. Still, there remained a few gaps. I have endeavored to draw as accurate a timeline as possible. Any errors or misinterpretations are mine alone.

Much deserved, I would like to thank my publishing team. First to my former Scholastic editor Cheryl Klein who gave me that little extra nudge at a critical time to pursue this story, then to Nick Thomas who brought his wonderful insight—and editing skills—to help me craft this story for young readers. Second to my agent and friend, Eric Lupfer, who is always there with steady guidance and cheerful encouragement, this book could not have happened with him. Thanks too to my film agent on the project, Ashley Fox, as well as the great folks at WME, Simon Trewin and Raffaella De Angelis. I also benefited from an early read by World War I aviation expert James Streckfuss. As always, my appreciation to the support of all of Scholastic, including Cian O'Day and the great Arthur Levine.

This book is dedicated to my long-time editor, Liz Hudson. We've been together now going on a decade and a half, and to be honest, I simply do not know how I'd do what I do without you at my side every step of the way. Thank you for your patience, insight, and crack-of-the-whip-but-with kindness. Sometimes I may not show it, but I know how lucky I am.

Finally, to Diane and our girls (and Moses thrown in for good measure). Words couldn't do justice in describing your impact in every part of my life!

BIBLIOGRAPHY

ARCHIVES

Australian War Memorial, Australia

British Library, UK

Bundesarchiv, Germany

Tasmanian State Archives, Australia

F. W. Harvey Collection, Gloucestershire Archives, UK

Archives and Special Collections, Hamilton Public Library, Canada

Prisoners of the First World War, ICRC Historical Archives, Switzerland

Imperial War Museum, UK

Liddle Collection, University of Leeds Special Collections, UK

Royal Air Force Museum, Hendon, UK

Sandwell Community History and Archives, UK

National Archives, Kew, UK

PERSONAL PAPERS

Bennett, Leonard J. (courtesy of Laurie Vaughan)

Blain, Cecil (courtesy of Hugh Lowe)

Clouston, Andrew (courtesy of Pete Clouston)

Dougall, Hector (courtesy of Brenda Merriman)

Gray, David (courtesy of Jane Gray)

Harvey, F. W. (courtesy of Gloucestershire Archives and the Harvey Family)

Kennard, Caspar (courtesy of C.A. Kennard and Diana Gillyatt)

Leggatt, E. W. (courtesy of Margaret Pretorius)

Lyon, Peter (courtesy of Louise Lyon)

Mallahan, Patrick (courtesy of Jacqueline Mallahan)

Morrogh, John (courtesy of Julyan Peard and Tony Wheatley)

Tullis, John K. (courtesy of Keil Tullis and Brian Tullis)

INTERVIEWS

Jane Gray

Laurie Vaughan

Diana Gillyatt

Hugh Lowe

BOOKS AND ARTICLES

Ackerley, J. R., *Escapers All: Being the Personal Narrative of Fifteen Escapers from War-Time Prison Camps, 1914–1918* (London: The Bodley Head, 1932)

Adam-Smith, Patsy, *Prisoners of War: From Gallipoli to Korea* (New York: Viking, 1997)

Afferbach, Holger and Strachan, Hew, *How Fighting Ends: A History of Surrender* (London: Oxford University Press, 2012)

Antrobus, H. A., *A History of the Jorehaut Tea Company Ltd.: 1859–1946* (London: Tea and Rubber Mail, 1948)

Barker, A. J., *The Bastard War: The Mesopotamian Campaign of 1914–18* (New York: Dial Press, 1967)

Barker, Ralph, *A Brief History of the Royal Flying Corps in World War I* (London: Constable & Robinson, 1995)

Barnes, A. F., *The Story of the 2/5th Battalion Gloucestershire Regiment, 1914–18* (Gloucester: Crypt House Press, 1930)

Bean, C. E. W., *Official History of Australia in the War of 1914–1918* (Sydney: Angus & Robertson, 1941)

Bills, Leslie Wm., *A Medal For Life: Biography of Captain Wm. Leefe Robinson* (Kent: Spellmount Limited, 1990)

Boden, Anthony, *F.W. Harvey: Soldier, Poet* (Gloucestershire: Sutton Publishing, 1988)

Bott, Alan, *An Airman's Outings* (London: Blackwood and Sons, 1917)

Bradbeer, Thomas, *Battle for Air Supremacy over the Somme* (Fort Leavenworth, KS: US Army Command and General Staff College, dissertation, 2004)

Bridges, Robert Seymour, *The Spirit of Man: An Anthology* (London: Longman, 1927)

Bryan, Tim, *The Great Western War 1939–1945* (London: Patrick Stephens, 1995)

Caunter, John Alan Lyde, *13 Days: The Chronicle of an Escape from a German Prison* (London: G. Bell and Sons, 1918)

Connes, George, *A POW's Memoir of the First World War: The Other Ordeal* (Oxford: Berg Publishers, 2004)

Cook, Jacqueline, *The Real Great Escape: The Story of the First World War's Most Daring Mass Breakout* (Sydney: Vintage Books, 2013)

Coombes, David, *Crossing the Wire: The Untold Stories of POWs in Battle and Captivity During WWI* (Wavell Heights Queensland: Big Sky Publishing, 2016)

Curtis, James, *James Whale: A New World of Gods and Monsters* (Minneapolis: University of Minnesota Press, 1998)

David, Saul, *100 Days to Victory: How the Great War Was Fought and Won 1914–1918* (London: Hodder & Stoughton, 2013)

Doegen, Wilhelm, *Kriegsgefangene Völker, Bd.: Der Kriegsgefangenen Haltung und Schicksal in Deutschland* (Berlin: Tafel, 1921)

Douglas, Sholto, *Years of Combat* (London: Collins, 1963)

Durnford, H. G., *The Tunnellers of Holzminden* (Cambridge University Press, 1920)

Ellis, John, *Eye-Deep in Hell: Trench Warfare in World War I* (New York: Pantheon Books, 1976)

Evans, A. J., *The Escaping Club* (London: Penguin Books, 1921)

Foot, M. R. D., Langley, James, *MI9: Escape and Evasion* (London: Bodley Head, 1979)

Fussell, Paul, *The Great War and Modern Memory* (New York: Oxford University Press, 2013)

Garrett, Richard, *P.O.W.: The Uncivil Face of War* (New York: David & Charles Publisher, 1981)

Gerard, James W., *My Four Years in Germany* (New York: Doran and Company, 1917)

Gilliland, Horace, *My German Prisons* (Boston: Houghton Mifflin, 1919)

Grider, John MacGavock, *War Birds: Diary of an Unknown Aviator* (College Station: Texas A&M Press, 1988)

Grinnell-Milne, *An Escaper's Log* (London: Bodley Head, 1926)

Guggisberg, F. G, *The Shop: The Story of the Royal Military Academy* (London: Cassell & Company, 1900)

Hanson, Neil, *Escape from Germany: The Greatest POW Break-Out of the First World War* (London: Corgi Books, 2011)

Harding, Geoffrey, *Escape Fever* (London: John Hamilton, 1935)

Hardy, J. L., *I Escape!* (London: Pen & Sword Military, 2014)

Hare, Paul R., *Fokker Fodder: The Royal Aircraft Factory B.E.2c* (Gloucestershire: Fonthill Media, 2014)

Hargreaves, Aura Kate, ed., *My Dearest, My Dearest: A War Story, a Love Story, a True Story of WWI by Those Who Lived It* (UK: Property People, 2014)

Harrison, M. C. C. & Cartwright, H. A., *Within Four Walls: A Classic of Escape* (London: Penguin Books, 1930)

Hart, Peter, *Somme Success: The Royal Flying Corps and the Battle of the Somme 1916* (London: Pen & Sword Books, 2001)

Harvey, F. W., *Comrades in Captivity: A Record of Life in Seven German Prison Camps* (London: Sidgwick & Jackson, 1920)

Hattersley, Roy, *The Edwardians* (London: Little Brown, 2004)

Hennebois, Charles, *In German Hands: The Diary of a Severely Wounded Prisoner* (London: William Heinemann, 1916)

Hervey, H. E., *Cage-Birds* (London: Penguin Books, 1940)

Herwig, Holger, *The First World War: Germany and Austria-Hungary 1914–1918* (London: Bloomsbury, 2014)

Hoffman, Conrad, *In the Prison Camps of Germany: A Narrative of "Y" Service among Prisoners of War* (New York: Association Press, 1920)

Horrocks, Brian, *Escape to Action* (New York: St. Martin's Press, 1960)

Hynes, Samuel, *The Edwardian Turn of Mind* (Princeton: Princeton University Press, 1968)

Jackson, Robert, *The Prisoners: 1914–18* (London: Routledge, 1989)

Jerrold, Douglas, *The Royal Naval Division* (London: Hutchinson & Company, 1923)

Jones, H. A., *The War in the Air: Being the Story of the part played in the Great War by the Royal Air Force*, Volume II (Oxford: Clarendon Press, 1928)

Jones, Heather, *Violence Against Prisoners of War in the First World War: Britain, France, and Germany, 1914–1920* (Cambridge University Press, 2011)

Keegan, John, *The First World War* (New York: Vintage Books, 2000)

Kieran, R. H., *Captain Albert Ball* (London: Aviation Book Club, 1939)

Knight, Gerald Featherstone, *'Brother Bosch', An Airman's Escape from Germany* (London: William Heinemann, 1919)

Krammer, Arnold, *Prisoners of War: A Reference Handbook* (London: Praeger Security International, 2008)

Lambert, Peter, *The Forgotten Airwar: Airpower in the Mesopotamian Campaign* (Fort Leavenworth, KS: Master's Thesis for US Army Command and General Staff College, 2012)

Lee, Arthur Gould, *Open Cockpit: A Pilot of the Royal Flying Corps* (London: Jarrolds, 1969)

Lewis-Stempel, John, *The War Behind the Wire: The Life, Death and Glory of British Prisoners of War, 1914–18* (London: Weidenfeld & Nicolson, 2014)

Lewis, Cecil, *Sagittarius Rising* (New York: Harcourt, Brace and Company, 1936)

Lewis, G. H., *Wings over the Somme, 1916–18* (Wrexham: Bridge Books, 1994)

Liddle, Peter, *The Airman's War: 1914–18* (London: Blanford Press, 1987)

Ludendorff, Erich, *My War Memories, 1914–1918,* Volume 1 (London: Hutchinson & Company, 1919)

MacDonald, Frank C., *The Kaiser's Guest* (Garden City, NY: Country Life Press, 1918)

McCarthy, Daniel J., *The Prisoner of War in Germany* (New York: Moffat, Yard, and Company, 1918)

Mitzkat, Jörg, *Stadt Holzminden und Umgebung Mitten im Weserbergland* (Holzminden: Jörg Mitzkat, 2016)

Money, R. R, *Flying and Soldiering* (London: Ivor Nicholson & Watson, 1936)

Morgan, J. H., translator, *The War Book of the German General Staff* (New York: McBride, Nast & Company, 1915)

Morton, Desmond, *Silent Battle: Canadian Prisoners of War in Germany: 1914–1919* (Toronto: Lester Publishing, 1992)

Moynihan, Michael, editor, *Black Bread and Barbed Wire* (London: Leo Cooper, 1978)

Neave, Airey, *Saturday at M.I.9: A History of Underground Escape Lines in North-West Europe in 1940–5 by a Leading Organiser at M.I. 9* (London: Leo Cooper, 1969)

Panayi, Panikos, *The Enemy in Our Midst: Germans in Britain during the First World War* (New York: Bloomsbury 1991)

Panayi, Panikos, *Prisoners of Britain: German Civilian and Combatant Internees during the First World War* (New York: Manchester University Press, 2012)

Peschardt, Lily, *The Letters of Jim Bennett: An Escapee of a WW1 German Prisoner of War Camp* (Unpublished Manuscript, Bennett Family Archives, 2015)

Phillimore, Godfrey, *Recollections of a Prisoner of War* (London: Edward Arnold & Co, 1930)

Repshire, J. Grant, "The Well-Loved Fields of Old": F. W. Harvey and Ivor Gurney's friendship and creative partnership during the First World War as seen through study of the F. W. Harvey Collection (*The Ivor Gurney Society Journal*, Vol. 20, 2014, pp. 7–30)

Schmitt, Margaret, "John Richard Cash: A Prisoner of War" (Unpublished manuscript, Imperial War Museum)

Sharma, Jayeeta, *Empire's Garden: Assam and the Making of India* (London: Duke University Press, 2011)

Shephard, Ben, *A War of Nerves: Soldiers and Psychiatrists in the Twentieth Century* (Cambridge: Harvard University Press, 2001)

Speed, Richard, *Prisoners, Diplomats, and the Great War: A Study in the Diplomacy of Captivity* (Westport, CT: Greenwood Press, 1990)

Spoerer, Mark, "The Mortality of Allied Prisoners of War and Belgian Civilian Deportees in German Custody during the First World War" (*Population Studies*, Vol. 60, 2006, pp. 121–36)

Thorn, J. C., *Three Years a Prisoner in Germany,* (Vancouver: Cowan and Brookhouse, 1919)

Thornton, R. K. R, ed., *Ivor Gurney War Letters* (Manchester: Carcanet New Press, 1983)

Tuchman, Barbara W., *The Guns of August: The Outbreak of World War I* (New York: Random House, 2014)

Vance, Jonathan F., *Objects of Concern: Canadian Prisoners of War through the Twentieth Century* (Seattle: University of Washington Press, 1994)

Vischer, A. L., *Barbed Wire Disease: A Psychological Study of the Prisoner of War* (London: John Bale and Sons, 1919)

von Richthofen, Manfred, *The Red Air Fighter* (London: The Aeroplane & General Publishing Company, 1917)

Warburton, Ernest, *Behind Boche Bars* (London: John Lane, 1920)

Waugh, Alec, *The Prisoners of Mainz* (New York: George Doran Company, 1918)

Weatherstone, John, *The Pioneers, 1825–1900, The Early British Tea and Coffee Planters and their Way of Life* (UK: Quiller, 1986)

Werner, Johannes, *Knight of Germany: Oswald Boelcke German Ace* (London: Casemate, 1991)

Whitehouse, Arch, *The Years of the Sky Kings* (New York: Curtis Books, 1959)

Winchester, Barry, *Beyond the Tumult* (New York: Charles Scribner's Sons, 1971)

Winter, Denis, *The First of the Few: Fighter Pilots of the First World War* (Athens, GA: University of Georgia Press, 1982)

Wise, S. F., *Canadian Airmen and the First World War: The Official History of the Royal Canadian Air Force*, Volume I (Toronto: University of Toronto Press, 1980)

Wyrall, Everard, *The Gloucestershire Regiment in the War 1914–1918* (London: Methuen & Co, 1931)

Yarnall, John, *Barbed Wire Disease: British & German Prisoners of War, 1914–19* (Gloucestershire: History Press, 2011)

NOTES

ABBREVIATIONS

AC—Family Papers of Andrew Clouston

AWM—Australian War Memorial, Australia

BA—Archives, British Library, UK

BARCH—Bundesarchiv, Germany

CHALK—Chalk Collection, Tasmanian State Archives, Australia

CK—Family Papers of Caspar Kennard

CWB—Family Papers of Cecil W. Blain

DBG—Family Papers of David B. Gray

GA—F. W. Harvey Collection, Gloucestershire Archives, UK

HFD—Family Papers of Hector F. Dougall

HPA—Colquohoun Family, Archives and Special Collections, Hamilton Public
   Library, Canada

ICRC—Prisoners of the First World War, ICRC Historical Archives,
   Switzerland

IWM—Imperial War Museum, UK

JDM—Family Papers of John D. Morrogh

JKT—Family Papers of John K. Tullis

LIDD—Liddle Collection, University of Leeds Special Collections, UK

LJB—Family Papers of Leonard J. Bennett

PM—Family Papers of Patrick Mallahan

RAF—Archival Collection, Royal Air Force Museum, Hendon, UK

SCHA—Private Papers of William Hugh Chance, Sandwell Community History
   and Archives, UK

TNA—National Archives, Kew, UK

"Stone walls do": Unpublished memoir. Papers of N. Birks. IWM.

A BIT OF HISTORY

Swept into this: Boden, p. 73.

"honor" and "glory": Tuchman, p. 113.

Although the murder: Keegan, pp. 16–87.

"world power or downfall": Tuchman, p. 14.

Many believed it: Horrocks, p. 15.

But by winter: Keegan, pp. 71–87; Tuchman, pp. 133, 185–09.

"Those vanquished in" Krammer, p. 3.

With the rise: Speed, p. 2.

"Like your own": Garrett, p. 28.

"sinkholes of filth": Krammer, p. 19.

"humanely treated" on: Report on Certain Violations of the Hague and Geneva
    Conventions. TNA: HO 45/10763/270829.

"a halcyon time" on: Speed, p. 5.

In the first six: Doegen, pp. 21–29; Jackson, p. 54.

Early in the: Panayi, *Prisoners of Britain*, p. 90; Speed, pp. 102–05.

In the act: Lewis-Stempel, p. xix.

The moans of: Gilliland, p. 9.

Those who reached: Lewis-Stempel, pp. 1–20. For a full account of the vagaries suffered
    by the British, John Lewis-Stempel's *The War Behind the Wire* is a wonderful study.

Roughly 80 percent: Lewis-Stempel, pp. 68–111; Spoerer, pp. 6–9.

According to one: Jones, p. 21.

"in case of overwhelming": Morgan, p. 97.

CHAPTER 1

The sky lightened: Unpublished memoir. Papers of Cecil Blain. IWM;
    Papers of W. Chance. IWM; Tullis Flight Log, 8/7/16. JKT.

"Contact!": Winter, pp. 91–92.

He sported a thick: Ibid, p. 87.

After his squadron: Winchester, pp. 1–2; Bott, p. 239.

For a moment: Lewis, Cecil, pp. 47–48.

"Open for us": Lee, pp. 5–6.

On July 1, 1916: Keegan, pp. 292–4.

As the five: Bott, p. 161; LIDD, p. 28; Money, p. 21.

A shell rocked: Winchester, p. 1.

The ancient city: Afferbach & Strachan, p. 294.

The planes broke: Blain, unpublished memoir. IWM; Statement Regarding
    Circumstances of Capture, David Griffiths. TNA: AIR 1/1207/204/5/2619;
    Winchester, pp. 4–5; 70th Squadron Report. TNA: AIR 1/2395/258/1.

"the introduction into": pamphlet: *The Diamond Jubilee*, SCHA: FP-CH 15/7/10.

"skill, energy and perseverance": Ibid.

"High spirits and resilience": Ibid, pp. 213–14.

The eldest son: Baptism Papers. CWB; Author interview with Hugh Lowe.

The outbreak of: Blain Service Records. TNA: AIR 76/41.

He did his flight: unpublished memoir. Papers of C. Roberts. LIDD: AIR-264;
    unpublished memoir. Papers of C. Illingworth. LIDD: AIR-170; Barker, *A Brief
    History of the RFC*, pp. 210–13; Winter, pp. 27–33.

On a typical: Skeet, Michael, "RFC Pilot Training," December 1998
    (www.theaerodrome.com).

Of the roughly: Exact figures on training deaths within the RFC remain difficult to
    determine. In Denis Winter's book, *The First of the Few*, he accounted that half
    of the "14,166 dead pilots" were killed in training (p. 36).

Blain survived: Blain Service Record. CWB.

That June: ibid; Blain Service Records. TNA: AIR 76/41.

He left for: Letter from Winchester to Miss Blain, March 3, 1969. CWB.

There was nothing: Blain, unpublished memoir. IWM; Winchester, pp. 4–6; 70th
    Squadron Report. TNA: AIR 1/2395/258/1; Bott, p. 254.

The Germans brought: Blain, unpublished memoir. IWM; Winchester, pp. 17–22.

CHAPTER 2

"There is to": Unpublished memoir. SCHA: FP-CH 15/7/8; Bott, pp. 32–33. The
    speech presented here is an amalgamation of these two versions, though
    primarily leaning on Bott's.

At Le Hameau: History of No. 11 Squadron. TNA: AIR 1/688/21/20/11.

"solid grey wool": Hart, pp. 169, 172.

"absolute master": Unpublished memoir. Papers of V. Coombs. LIDD: POW-016.

Air crews were: Barker, *A Brief History of the RFC*, p. 171.

What the crews: Werner, pp. 1–7, 148–52, 199–201, 230–34.

At their aerodromes: Unpublished memoirs. Papers of F. Morris, RAF; Hart, pp. 152–53.

Gray reviewed his: Report from Captain Gray, August 21, 1918. TNA: AIR 1/501/15/333/1.

Gray had spent: Family Records. DBG; Antrobus, pp. 145–53.

He settled early: Family Records. DBG; Guggisberg, pp. 237–50.

Upon graduation: Service Record of D. B. Gray, British Indian Army Records, BA.

"A capable and efficient": Ibid.

Gray also sank: Interview with Jane Gray. For reference, "Munshi" is originally a Persian word for secretary or writer, but in India, it was used to identify language teachers who taught the British.

In spring 1915: Lambert, pp. 45–60.

Later that year: Author interview with Jane Gray; Kieran, pp. 60–91.

After earning his: Family Records. DBG; Service Record of D. B. Gray, British Indian Army Records, BA; TNA: AIR 76/192.

After a dismal: Unpublished memoir. SCHA: FP-CH 15/7/8; Money, pp. 100–04; Winchester, pp. 6–11.

Before crossing the: *The Destonian*, June 1918.

Suddenly, the sky: Letter from David Gray to Mrs. Morris, November 25, 1916. Papers of F. Morris, RAF; Report from Captain Gray, August 21, 1918. TNA: AIR 1/501/15/333/1; Werner, pp. 240–242; von Richthofen, pp. 74–78; Report on Capture of Leonard Helder. TNA: WO 339/11209.

"You are my": Winchester, p. 11.

Gray was quiet: Ibid., p. 28.

"The war is over": Unpublished memoir. SCHA: FP-CH 15/7/8; Money, p. 106.

The following morning: Money, pp. 105–110; Tullis, unpublished memoir. JKT; letter from David Gray to Mrs. Morris, November 25, 1916.

CHAPTER 3

Caspar Kennard's first: Letter from Caspar Kennard to Chris Kennard, October 13, 1916. CK; letter from C. Kennard to his parents. October 12, 1916. Papers of C. Kennard. IWM; "Shot Down Behind Enemy Lines," news clipping, undated. Papers of C. Kennard. IWM.

He had only: Pilot logbook. Papers of C. Kennard. IWM.

Seven months before: Author interview with Diana Gillyatt; Kennard Family Papers. CK.

After earning his: Kennard Service Records. TNA: AIR 76/271.

"Somewhere behind the": Letter from C. Kennard to his parents. October 12, 1916. Papers of C. Kennard. IWM.

Days later, their: Winchester, p. 36.

When he was: Report by Gerald Knight. TNA: FO 383/272; Money, pp. 114–15; Winchester, p. 36.

A guard brought: Blain, unpublished memoir. IWM; Report on Prisoners Camp at Osnabrück. TNA: FO 383/267.

The British Red: Hanson, pp. 106, 113–18.

In early November: Blain, unpublished memoir. IWM.

Everyone at Osnabrück: Ibid; Winchester, pp. 37–38.

"My dearest Mother": Blain, unpublished memoir. IWM.

"Will they twig": Ibid.

While they waited: Letters from Hugh Chance to his family. October–November, 1916. SCHA: FP-CH 15/7/3; Money, pp. 116–19; diary, October 5–November 30, 1916. SCHA: FP-CH 15/7/8.

Every day: Winchester, pp. 38–41.

"Dear old Mum": Ibid.

In early December: Tullis, unpublished memoir. JKT.

Then, on December: David Gray. ICRC.

CHAPTER 4

Two months passed: Blain, unpublished memoir. IWM; Tullis, unpublished memoir. JKT; Chance, unpublished memoir. SCHA: FP-CH 15/7/8.

"evil swine": Blain, unpublished memoir. IWM.

"Ready?": Winchester, p. 44.

"Help! The English": Blain, unpublished memoir. IWM. Knight, p. 49.

"Yes.": Blain, unpublished memoir. IWM.

Blankenstein decided to: Knight, pp. 50–54.

"Raus!": Ibid, p. 51; Letters from Hugh Chance to his family. March–April, 1917. SCHA: FP-CH 15/7/5.

After a couple: Lewis-Stempel, p. 122; Letters from Hugh Chance to his family. March–April 1917. SCHA: FP-CH 15/7/5; Tullis, unpublished memoir. JKT.

Surrounding it now: Evans, pp. 19–21.

"cunning attack": "Begalubigte Abschrift," April 7, 1917. Papers of C. Kennard, RAF.

They spent it: Blain, unpublished memoir. IWM; Tullis, unpublished memoir. JKT.

CHAPTER 5

Captain David Gray: Winchester, p. 103. In his book, *Beyond the Tumult*, Winchester references this escape to have taken place during June 1917. At this time, Gray would have been at his next camp, Schwarmstadt. That said, it is clear this escape was attempted from Crefeld, and given the weather and window of opportunity, spring was its most likely time.

With its warm: Report on Crefeld. Bundesarchiv 901/84359; Letter from Burlow to his mother, April 14, 1917. Papers of R. Burrows. LIDD: POW-010.

Holding some 800: Report by Lieutenant Russell. TNA: FO 383/275; Phillimore, pp. 44–49; unpublished memoir. Papers of L. McNaught-Davis. LIDD: POW-043.

Nevertheless, Gray was: The Crefeld Secret Inquiry. Winchester. Appendix II.

With Crefeld only: Winchester, pp. 104–105.

In the months: unpublished memoir. Papers of J. Dykes. IWM; January–May 1917. diary. Papers of D. Grant. IWM; Caunter, pp. 27, 38; unpublished memoir. Papers of L. McNaught-Davis. LIDD: POW-043.

After a long: Winchester, pp. 105–16.

CHAPTER 6

The pigs' squeals: Evans, p. 41; Clausthal Report. BARCH: R 901/84348. For note: Some accounts have the Clausthal commandant named Wolfe, others Puttenson. There are similar discrepancies between reports and prisoner memoirs at many of the camps.

Commandant Wolfe: Clausthal Report. BARCH: R 901/84348; Statement by Lieutenant Anderson. Papers of F. Mann. IWM; Knight, p. 71.

Still, compared to: Blain, unpublished memoir. IWM; Money, p. 128.

The prisoners made: Unpublished memoir. Papers of A. Martin-Thomson. IWM.

It began with: Blain, unpublished memoir. IWM; Report on Visit to Detention
    Camp at Clausthal. TNA: FO 383/270.

"Are all Canadians": Spectator, December 5, 1966; a series of undated newspaper
    clippings, HPA.

One day, in: Knight, pp. 78–81.

Blain and Kennard: Blain, unpublished memoir. IWM.

CHAPTER 7

As the fall: "Draft of an Agreement between British and German Governments,"
    July 1917. TNA: CAB 24/19/39.

"prisoner's Mecca": Durnford, p. 15.

They did not: Letter from Barlow to his parents, September 26, 1917. Papers of
    A. Barlow. LIDD: POW-002.

"the face of": Cook, p. 176.

Private-school: "The First Great Escape," *Cross & Cockade* (Spring 2016).

As a POW: Rathborne Account. TNA: AIR 1/7/726/129/1; Report by Rathborne.
    TNA: WO 161/96.

It was after: Durnford, pp. 18–21; Hargreaves, p. 193.

The former infantry: Report on Conditions of Officers' Camps in Xth Army Corps.
    TNA: FO 383/399; unpublished memoir. Papers of R. Gough. LIDD: POW-029.

"glad to see": Durnford, p. 19.

"bedroom candles and": Ibid.

They were divided: Letter, June 16, 1918. Papers of L. Nixon. IWM.

When the morning: Durnford, pp. 19–21; Report on Conditions of Officers' Camps
    in Xth Army Corps. TNA: FO 383/399.

"you wouldn't get": Warburton, p. 96.

"cad": Report on Conditions of Officers' Camps in Xth Army Corps. TNA: FO
    383/399; Notes on Holzminden. Papers of M. Pannett. IWM.

"had been enough": Hanson, p. 74.

CHAPTER 8

The prison was: *The Spectator*, May 19, 1928; unpublished memoir. Papers of
R. Gough. LIDD: POW-029; Ackerley, p. 78; diary, October 14, 1917. Papers of
D. Grant. IWM; Notes. Papers of M. Pannett. IWM; Hanson, pp. 43–45.

Two prisoners recently: Thorn, p. 65. In his memoir, Thorn offers a compelling
portrait of this early escape at Holzminden, not to mention one of life in the
camps. Well worth a read.

The two barracks: Unpublished memoir. Papers of R. Gough. LIDD: POW-029;
Durnford, pp. 52–60; September 28, 1917. Diary. Papers of D. Grant. IWM.

Thorn and Wilkins: Thorn, pp. 66–68; unpublished memoir. Papers of L.
McNaught-Davis. LIDD: POW-043; Rathborne Account. TNA: AIR
1/7/726/129/1; Garland, Edgar, "My Dashes for Freedom," *Wide World
Magazine*, June 1919.

"had left the": Thorn, p. 87.

Bloodhounds were brought: Ibid, pp. 87–88; Hanson, pp. 15–52.

The Poldhu relayed: Report by Alan Wilken. TNA: WO 161/96; Clausthal Camp,
Diary and Comments. SCHA: FP-CH 15/7/5.

The prisoners now: Durnford, pp. 24–25; report by A. E. Haig, January 20, 1918.
Papers of A. Haig. IWM.

"barbarians": Report by Captain F.B. Binney. TNA: WO 161/96; Report by Samuel
Ellis. TNA: WO 161/96.

Back in his: Report by Samuel Ellis. TNA: WO 161/96; Report on Conditions of
Officers' Camps in Xth Army Corps. TNA: FO 383/399.

As some of: October 1917. Diary. Papers of J. Chapman RAF; letter in Code
Despatched from Holzminden, October 9, 1917. TNA: FO 383/275; Horrocks,
p. 21.

Throughout October: Letter from Bennett to his mother, October 17, 1917. LJB;
report on Holzminden, November 22, 1917. TNA: FO 383/275; report by
A. E. Haig, January 20, 1918. Papers of A. Haig. IWM.

"I had nothing": Report by Lieutenant Insall. TNA: FO 383/272.

"Look at these": Horrocks, p. 26; *Auckland Star*, March 22, 1919; Durnford,
pp. 16–23; unpublished memoir. Papers of A. Barlow. LIDD: POW-002;
Warburton, pp. 91–97; *Sydney Mail*, August 6, 1919.

There they quickly: October 1917. Diary. Papers of D. Grant. IWM; Letter in Code
    Despatched from Holzminden, October 9, 1917. TNA: FO 383/275;
    unpublished memoir. Papers of L. McNaught-Davis. LIDD: POW-043.

CHAPTER 9

"Get up": Unpublished memoir. Papers of R. Gough. LIDD: POW-029.

"Cost price": Durnford, p. 37.

Since arriving at: Unpublished memoir. Papers of L. McNaught-Davis. LIDD:
    POW-043; Report on Conditions of Officers' Camps in Xth Army Corps. TNA:
    FO 383/399.

Waiting was one: Harvey, p. 228.

The little tyrannies: unpublished memoir. Papers of L. McNaught-Davis. LIDD:
    POW-043; report by Lieutenant Purves. TNA: FO 383/399.

"When a more": Harvey, p. 227.

Theft was pervasive: Notes on Holzminden. Papers of M. Pannett. IWM; letter from
    Nixon. Papers of L. Nixon. IWM.

For no reason: Letter to Nixon family. Papers of L. Nixon. IWM.

"Time drags slowly": Coombes (Kindle location 5217).

"The wearisome sameness": Lewis-Stempel, pp. 117–18.

Second Lieutenant William: Harvey, pp. 170–71.

In late October: Report on Holzminden, November 1917. BARCH: R 85/4337;
    unpublished memoir. Papers of L. McNaught-Davis. LIDD: POW-043; Garland,
    Edgar, "My Dashes for Freedom," *Wide World Magazine*, June 1919.

The barricades in: Hanson, pp. 167–68.

The Holzminden inmates: Newsclip, "Bucks Officer's Adventures in Germany,"
    undated. Papers of J. Shaw. IWM.

"You see, gentleman": Durnford, p. 50.

Private Dick Cash: unpublished memoir. Papers of D. Morrish. LIDD: ADD-001;
    unpublished memoir. Papers of J. Dykes. IWM.

When war broke: Schmitt. IWM

He lived with: Hanson, pp. 49–53.

At 7 a.m.: Unpublished memoir. Papers of J. Dykes. IWM.

"Taking the officers": Ibid.

Dick Cash, with: Schmitt. IWM

CHAPTER 10

Shorty Colquhoun wanted: Ackerley, p. 78.

Finding the best: Recollections of L. J. Bennett, oral history, LIDD; Durnford, pp.
71–75; Hanson, pp. 183–85; "The Holzminden Tunnellers Want to Meet Again,"
Answers, June 11, 1938.

He recruited his: Letter from Bennett to Lyon, May 13, 1938. LJB.

First they would: Recollections of L. J. Bennett, oral history, LIDD; Tullis,
unpublished memoir. JKT.

The next day: Ackerley, pp. 78–79; Recollections of L. J. Bennett, Oral History,
LIDD; Tullis, unpublished memoir. JKT. Although the record on this critical
scouting mission was clear, the two individuals responsible remained
unmentioned in all accounts on Holzminden. Given the intricate engineering of
the slide panel, and the experience of the Pink Toes, namely Moysey and Rogers,
in creating such a contraption, the author surmised these two were responsible.

One of them: *New Zealand Herald*, August 27, 1938.

A bribe of: Hanson, pp. 194–95.

On November 5: Rathborne Account. TNA: AIR 1/7/726/129/1; November 5,
1917. Diary. Papers of J. Chapman, RAF.

"eye-wash": Harding, p. 92.

The men tried: Report on Holzminden, November 1917. BARCH: R 85/4337

"could be obviated": Report on Holzminden. BARCH: R 85/4337.

"professionally incapable": Letter from British Vice Consulate, May 16, 1917. TNA:
FO 383/270.

"The first officer": Letter in code, November 12, 1917. TNA: FO 383/275.

"Holzminden was an": Letter from W.R.C. Green. Papers of R. Burrows. LIDD:
POW-010.

Lord Newton had: Summary of Reprisals Taken by British and German
Governments. TNA: CAB 24/6/375; meeting minutes. October 26, 1917. TNA:
FO 383/273.

CHAPTER 11

There was never: Cook, pp. 20–21.

Niemeyer continued: Report by A. E. Haig, January 20, 1918. Papers of A. Haig. IWM.

The greatest revenge: Ibid, p. 230.

On one of: Durnford, pp. 71–88.

One orderly stood: Tullis, unpublished memoir. JKT.

"All clear": Durnford, p. 79.

Gray and his: *Australian*, March 3, 1922.

Thin lines of: Durnford, pp. 71–88.

Using spoons and: *Sunday Express*, May 8, 1938; Morrogh, unpublished memoir.
　　JDM; recollections of L. J. Bennett, oral history, LIDD.

At first, they: *Australian*, March 3, 1922.

At Christmas, Colquhoun: Durnford, p. 75.

The men sang: December 1917. Diary. Papers of D. Grant. IWM; Hanson, p. 200.

The following morning: Unpublished memoir. Papers of L. McNaught-Davis.
　　LIDD: POW-043.

But into this: Notes. Papers of M. Pannett. IWM; Durnford, p. 75; J. W. Shaw, "The
　　Holzminden Escape Tunnel." News clipping. Papers of J. Shaw. IWM.

Caspar Kennard wriggled: Winchester, p. 112. According to Winchester, Kennard
　　joined the project tunnel in January 1918. Kennard left no record of the exact
　　date, but in his archival files, he was clearly working with Gray at this point in
　　bribing a Holzminden dentist for supplies. Gerichtsschreiber des Landgerichts
　　Brief, January 18, 1918. Papers of C. Kennard, RAF. Given Kennard's arrest and
　　imprisonment from escape, this timeline figures well.

On reaching the: Harding, pp. 135–39; Shaw, J.W., "The Holzminden Escape
　　Tunnel." News clipping. Papers of J. Shaw. IWM; Unpublished memoir. Papers
　　of W. English, RAF.

CHAPTER 12

They filled their: Hanson, pp. 136–41.

"There was a": V. Coombs, oral history interview. IWM.

Besides actors, the: Hanson, pp. 136–39.

James Whale, who: Curtis, pp. 15–26.

"Pots of paint": James Whale, "Our Life at Holzminden," *Wide World Magazine*,
　　undated. Papers of J. Whale. IWM.

"a motley crew": Unpublished memoir. Papers of G. Gilbert, RAF.

The arrival in: Letter from M. R. Chidson, May 15, 1936. Medlicott family papers. http://www.fam.medlicott.uk.com/HEM_files/7_HWMedlicott.html. Cook, p. 151.

A legend to: Evans, p. 56.

At 3:30 p.m.: Ibid; Durnford, pp. 60–63; Letter from M. R. Chidson, May 15, 1936. Medlicott family papers. http://www.fam.medlicott.uk.com/HEM_files/7 _HWMedlicott.html. Unpublished memoir. Papers of J. Cash. IWM; February 1918. Diary. Papers of D. Grant. IWM.

"All my boys": Unpublished memoir. Papers of N. Birks. IWM.

When the officers: Report on Conditions of Officers' Camps in Xth Army Corps. TNA: FO 383/399.

"unblemished record": Durnford, p. 63.

"it was impossible": Letter from M. R. Chidson, May 15, 1936. Medlicott family papers. http://www.fam.medlicott.uk.com/HEM_files/7_HWMedlicott.html.

In late February: Durnford, p. 95.

Since the Boxing: December 1917–February 1918. Diary. Papers of D. Grant. IWM.

Rather than welcoming: Lewis Stempel, pp. 246–247.

"I felt like": Vance, p. 68.

At the end: Harvey, pp. 239–240.

They left: *King Country Chronicle*, September 27, 1919; TNA: ADM 273/23/137; Morrogh, unpublished memoir. JDM.

Blain clawed the: Blain, unpublished memoir. IWM; Recollections of L. J. Bennett, oral history, LIDD.

At last, he: Blain, unpublished memoir. IWM.

Back by the: Recollections of L. J. Bennett, oral history, LIDD; Tullis, unpublished memoir. JKT.

Kennard stood just: Durnford, pp. 96–99.

CHAPTER 13

Whether walking in: Harvey, pp. 142–43.

There was a: Speech Notes. AC; Tullis, unpublished memoir. JKT.

"black gusts of": Hanson, pp. 79–80.

"Letter Boy," the: David, p. 442; Durnford, pp. 81–85; Mallahan, P. "The Big Breakout." Unpublished article. PM.

"I do not": Durnford, pp. 84–85.

With his photography: Schmitt. IWM

Each week, Gray: Rathborne account. TNA: AIR 1/7/726/129/1; Tullis, unpublished memoir. JKT.

"We must be": Harvey, p. 135.

"accidentally": Tullis, unpublished memoir. JKT.

In mid-May: Notes. Papers of M. Pannett. IWM; summary of Reprisals Taken by British and German Governments. TNA: CAB 24/6/375.

At first the: Durnford, pp. 108–10; Morrogh, unpublished memoir. JDM.

"Yes, they are": Ibid, p. 289.

"sudden dash": Letter from M. R. Chidson, May 15, 1936.
http://www.fam.medlicott.uk.com/HEM_files/7_HWMedlicott.html.

Then, while several: Grinnell-Milne, pp. 303–304.

The tunnelers in: Hargreaves, p. 392.

Nobody lived in: Ibid, pp. 109–13; Papers of M. Pannett. IWM; Rathborne account. TNA: AIR 1/7/726/129/1.

CHAPTER 14

A lunatic who: Winchester, pp. 142–44.

Gray would be: Forged document. Papers of C. Kennard, RAF.

"We hereby certify": Günther note. Papers of C. Kennard, RAF.

One officer's escape: J. K. Bousfield, "An Exciting Escape from a German Prisoners' of War Camp," *Caian: The Magazine of Gonville and Caius College* (undated).

"Bone dry": Tullis, unpublished memoir. JKT; notes. AC.

"true German style": Rathborne account. TNA: AIR 1/7/726/129/1.

On June 6: Diary, June 6, 1918. HFD.

Sutcliffe, whose nickname: Harvey, pp. 237–38; Durnford, pp. 120–24.

Compounding this anxiety: Document from Holland, Harsh Treatment of Captain Robinson. TNA: FO 383/399; Report by Ortweiler. TNA: WO 161/96.

"simple disobedience": "Court martial of David B. Gray, June 12, 1918. TNA: FO 383/401; Durnford, p. 119.

CHAPTER 15

Jim Bennett: Notes on Holzminden, Papers of M. Pannett. IWM.

The 26-year-old: Bennett and Tullis interview, LJB: Author interview with Laurie Bennett.

"last lap": Durnford, p. 118.

On June 30: Rathbone account. TNA: AIR 1/7/726/129/1; Tullis, unpublished memoir. JKT; Bennett, "A Little Introduction Speech," LJB.

"nosed its way." Recollections of L. J. Bennett, oral history, LIDD.

They had no: Morrogh, unpublished memoir. JDM; Notes. Papers of M. Pannett. IWM.

The other restrictions: McPhail, Angus. His Book Holzminden. LJB.

"Are you in": Ackerley, p. 75.

"Expecting something big": Diary. July 1918. HFD.

Livewire reluctantly agreed: Durnford, p. 129.

Gray led the: Durnford, pp. 124–27; *King County Chronicle*, September 27, 1919. Garland reinforces that Gray was in charge of the plan, and who should go where/when during the night of the breakout.

The first escape: Bousfield, J.K., "An Exciting Escape."

They drew up: Papers of M. Pannett. IWM; Blain, unpublished memoir. IWM.

Two officers volunteered: Recollections of L. J. Bennett, oral history, LIDD.

The next night: Durnford, pp. 129–30.

CHAPTER 16

"*Tonight!*" All through: Freeman, James, "The Holzminden Tunnelers Want to Meet Again," *Answers*, June 11, 1938; July 21–24, diary. HFD.

At 6 p.m.: Durnford, pp. 131–32.

"Holzminden—Escaped July": Winchester, p. 152.

"Oh, shut up": Ibid, p. 154.

Throughout Block B: Morrogh, unpublished memoir. JDM.

Jim Bennett was: Recollections of L. J. Bennett, oral history, LIDD.

"wonderfully Teutonic": Durnford, pp. 132–33.

No matter how: Ackerley, pp. 84–86.

"finale of a": Gore, Max, "The Long Dim Tunnel." CHALK.

A religious man: *News Chronicle*, July 24, 1948; Butler account, as quoted in Durnford, pp. 159–60.

Minutes before the: Hanson, pp. 263–64.

They were depending: Letter from Ernest Collinson to Bennett, May 25, 1938. LJB; Ernest Collinson Record, ICRC.

"Don't bother, Collinson": Winchester, pp. 157–58.

CHAPTER 17

"Chocks away": Winchester, pp. 158–59.

During one stretch: Blain, unpublished memoir. IWM.

"What's up?":Winchester, pp. 160–61.

Sixty yards away: Tullis, unpublished memoir. JKT.

Taking care anyway: Blain, unpublished memoir. IWM.

At last he: Morrogh, unpublished memoir. JDM.

In the distance: Foot, p. 18.

"Bet Niemeyer": Winchester, pp. 161–63; Blain, unpublished memoir. IWM.

Charles Rathborne thrust: Rathborne account. TNA: AIR 1/7/726/129/1.

Jim Bennett was: Bennett, "A Little Introduction Speech," LJB; J. K. Bousfield, "An Exciting Escape."

After over an: Rathborne account. TNA: AIR 1/7/726/129/1.

"Your turn, Major": Morrogh, unpublished memoir. JDM; letter from Tony Wheatley to author, August 20, 1916; Senan Molony, "Titanic: The Last Photograph," April 23, 2004. Published online: https://www.encyclopedia -titanica.org/titanic-the-last-photograph.html.

"All clear," an: Morrogh, unpublished memoir. JDM.

CHAPTER 18

David Gray scanned: Winchester, pp. 163–68. Barry Winchester provides the best account of the run to Holland by Gray, Kennard, and Blain. His description is backed up by the maps.

"huge crocodile": Blain, unpublished memoir. IWM.

There was trouble: Notes. Papers of L. Nixon. IWM.

"What's the idea?": Garland, "My Dashes to Freedom."

Twenty-nine officers: Letter from C.A. Lyon to Bennett, May 17, 1938, LJB;
The Australian, March 3, 1922.

Back at the: Garland, "My Dashes to Freedom."

Soon after, Hartigan: Unpublished memoir. Papers of R. Gough. LIDD: POW-029;
notes on Holzminden. Papers of M. Pannett. IWM.

"So, a tunnel": Durnford, p. 139.

"The tunnel has": "The Moles of Holzminden," Popular Flying, December 1938.

"Neun und zwanzig": News clipping, undated. Papers of
F.W. Harvey, GA.

"Niemeyer's jaw dropped": Durnford, p. 139.

Then the commandant: Unpublished memoir. Papers of
R. Gough. LIDD: POW-029; Report by Lt. Ortweiler. TNA: WO 161/96;
July 25, 1918. Diary. HFD.

CHAPTER 19

Hunkered in corn: Bennett, "A Little Introduction Speech," LJB; Bousfield, J. K.,
"An Exciting Escape."

The hunt was: Tullis, unpublished memoir. JKT.

"full view of": Morrogh, unpublished memoir. JDM.

Heavy rucksacks digging: Winchester, pp. 175–77.

They stopped, and: Günther note. Papers of C. Kennard, RAF.

He was furious: Statement by Lieutenant Ortweiler. TNA: WO 161/96; Harvey, pp.
241–42; Coombs, V.C., "Sixty Years On," Royal Air Forces Quarterly, Summer
1976; July 26, 1918. Diary. HFD.

"We urgently request": Täglicher Anzeiger (Holzminden), August 2, 1918.

The reward offered: Bennett, "A Little Introduction Speech," LJB.

On the afternoon: Rathborne account. TNA: AIR 1/7/726/129/1.

After their antics: Winchester, pp. 178–80.

CHAPTER 20

For the next: Rathborne account. TNA: AIR 1/7/726/129/1.

In Bebra: Speech Notes. Officer POW Dining Club. LIDD: POW-072.

He slept fitfully: Rathborne account. TNA: AIR 1/7/726/129/1; Herwig, p. 288.

On their own: Durnford, pp. 143–47; July 24–August 3, 1918. Diary. HFD.

Never one to: Durnford, p. 145.

By looking at: *Täglicher Anzeiger* (Holzminden), August 2, 1918.

"Having a lovely time": "The Men Who Dug a Tunnel," *Evening Standard*, July 24, 1958.

CHAPTER 21

Dogs were barking: Winchester, pp. 182–83.

They had rations: Letter from Cita Kennard, August 1918. CK.

Due south of: Winchester, pp. 182–185.

Southwest of Blenheim: Bennett & Tullis interview. LJB.

Armed sentries patrolled: Caunter, pp. 209–13; Gilliland, p. 230.

By observing the: Bennett, "A Little Introduction Speech," LJB.

"*Halt!*": Recollections of L. J. Bennett, oral history, LIDD.

CHAPTER 22

On the morning: Escape Route Map. Papers of C. Kennard, RAF, Winchester, pp. 184–85.

At twilight, they: Letter from Cita Kennard, August 1918, CK.

The three airmen: Winchester, pp. 185–88.

The three soon: Winchester, pp. 185–88.

What kept them: Blain, unpublished memoir. IWM.

It was approaching: Cypher telegram from Rotterdam, August 8, 1918. TNA: FO 383/381.

They crept slowly: Winchester, pp. 185–88.

"Duck!" he warned: Ibid, p. 187.

Together they yawped: Letter from Blain to Uncle Hugh, August 28, 1918; Letter from Cita Kennard, August 1918. CK.

"Escaped and arrived": Telegram from Kennard, August 1918. Papers of
    C. Kennard, RAF.

Secret cables from: Return to UK of British Prisoners-of-war Escaped from
    Germany, August 7, 1918. TNA: FO 383/381.

"British Prisoners Dig": *New York Times,* August 7, 1918.

On the evening: Cypher Telegram, August 7, 1918. TNA: FO 383/381; Harrison, p. 183.

The following morning: Tullis, unpublished memoir. JKT.

From the window: Gilliland, pp. 256–59.

"take three months'": Harrison, p. 183.

"The Queen joins": Letter to Blain, 1918. CWB.

"The Tunnel to": *Daily Sketch*, December 18, 1918.

"Daring Escape": *Evening Express*, August 26, 1918.

Despite all the: Service Record of D. B. Gray, British Indian Army Records, BA;
    Money, p. 151; Service Record of C. Blain. CWB.

CHAPTER 23

In the period: Cypher telegram from Netherland, August 24, 1918. TNA: FO
    383/399; Durnford, pp. 146–54; statement by M.S. Fryer. TNA: FO 383/400.

Continued escape attempts: August–September 1918. Diary. HFD.

"conspiring to destroy": Hanson, pp. 300–04.

Deciding that the: Beglsubigte Abschrift. Papers of R.M. Paddison. LIDD:
    POW-049.

"having made an": Schmitt. IWM

But with 250,000: Herwig, p. 403.

"They would all": September 29–October 2, 1918. Diary. HFD.

He stayed mostly: Durnford, p. 159.

"always done all": *New York Times*, December 15, 1918.

"You see, I": *New York Times*, December 15, 1918.

"The war is": "A Parting Word." Pamphlets for repatriates. IWM.

Yet this farewell: Unpublished memoir. Papers of R. Gough. LIDD: POW-029;
    December 9–10, 1918. Diary. HFD.

"awe, envy, and": James Whale, "Our Life at Holzminden," *Wide World Magazine*,
    undated. Papers of J. Whale. IWM.

EPILOGUE

Twenty years after: Holzminden Tunnel, Twentieth Anniversary Dinner pamphlet. JKT.

"gallant and able": Letter from keeper of the privy purse, February 5, 1919. CWB.

"His untimely death": "Prisoners in Germany," unsourced newsclip, March 9, 1935. Papers of C. Kennard. IWM.

"enemy officers": Hanson, p. 329.

"I know damn": Ibid, p. 337.

When he had: Author interview with Jane Gray.

During World War II: Foot, pp. 22–26; historical record of I.S.9. TNA: WO 208/3242; history of intelligence school No. 9. TNA: WO 208/3246.

"improbable but possible": Notes, Bennett MI9 lecture. LJB.

By one historian's: Lewis-Stempel, pp. 190–91.

In contrast before: Foot, p. 5, Appendix I. As Foot and Langley admit, these numbers are but a best-guess approximation.

"Do as you": Author interview with Laurie Vaughan.

PHOTO CREDITS

INDEX

Note: Page numbers in *italics* refer to illustrations.

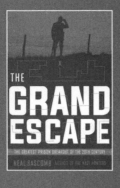